DISASTER MANUAL FOR FINANCIAL RECOVERY

A SELF HELP GUIDE
TO RECEIVE THE
MOST DISASTER FUNDS

ROBERT WINTER

DISCLAIMER

This book is a memoir based on certain events, locales and conversations from the author's memories of them. In order to maintain the anonymity of individuals and places, some identifying characteristics and details such as physical properties, occupations and places of residence have been changed, and in some instances the people, places and stories portrayed do not in any way alter the outcome of any material portion of this text.

ISBN-13:978-0-9964229-2-5
ISBN-10:0996422927

PRINTED IN THE UNITED STATES OF AMERICA

HTTP://WWW.DUSTINTHEWINDFEMABOOK.COM

FOLLOW ROBERT WINTER AT:

DustInTheWindfemabook.com

Facebook.com/dustinthewindFEMAbook

Instagram/Femadude15

Twitter.com/@DustInTheWindBk

YouTube.com/FRECKSZONE

Celebrities4DisasterRelief.org

Email: FEMADUDE15@aol.com

"Insurance isn't the best answer,
it is the only answer, but the right coverage is imperative!"

~Frecks Smart quote

This book is dedicated to the victims of disaster,
who are always on my mind.

Table of Contents

WHY THIS MANUAL IS SO IMPORTANT

You have probably heard the drumbeat of disturbing news reports and seen the endless parade of alarming headlines over the past years, especially lately with the Texas floods this summer. We live in the most unpredictable of times and see behind the headlines, the depth of the challenges that we confront.

Most weather experts predict that over the next decade, the hurricanes will be more powerful, the storms more frequent and severe, with fires more deadly as global warming patterns continue to alter our way of life and our relationship to nature.

Some international groups on global warming have stated several times that North America will experience more hurricanes, floods, droughts, heat waves and wildfires while the coastlines will be swamped by rising sea levels. The human lives lost, economic impacts felt and the social disruptions will be enormous.

With the warnings now so frequent and so clear, people must be preparing themselves, RIGHT?

WRONG! Despite the lessons of Katrina, Rita, Ike, Sandy and other devastating hurricanes, one-third of all the people living in high-risk areas say they will ignore future evacuation orders. These studies have been done along the coast from Texas to North Carolina, some of the most high risk areas in America for hurricanes. The findings were unbelievable that people view their homes as safe and evacuating as dangerous with most of them planning on staying. And with most believing they would be rescued if they needed to be. Hey, they see it on television all the time with people being rescued!

Other alarming information is that two out or three people in high risk areas DO NOT even have an agreed upon meeting place in the event their family is separated during a disaster. Half of them DO NOT have $300 in cash on hand to use if they need to evacuate and if public services, such as ATM machines, are no longer functioning. One quarter of them DO NOT own a first aid kit. Over 70 percent in hurricane prone areas don't have a survival plan.

Even in the aftermath of Katrina, Rita, Ike and Sandy, most of these people have not prepared a survival kit, planned evacuation routes or secured adequate insurance. They are still depending on government agencies to keep them safe and to rescue them. After Katrina, do you really feel safe knowing FEMA is going to come to the rescue and save you? How many of those people who are no longer with us because of that storm thought that as well?

Examining the Katrina disaster, a storm long predicted by weather experts, PBS created a documentary entitled *The Storm*, an hour-long FRONTLINE investigation[1] into how every branch of the government, from local to state to federal, stood unprepared, overwhelmed and in chaos in the summer of 2005 when the hurricane struck, killing over 900 people in New Orleans alone and causing over 1,800 deaths overall.

The last disaster of that magnitude occurred four years earlier with 9/11. Weren't any lessons learned about communication standards during those four years between first responders, local, state and federal governments and its agencies?

How about when the next earthquake hits? More than likely, with all the quakes around the world, it's going to be BIG. We haven't had a Loma Prieta or Northridge quake in over 20 years and be assured, the pressure is building on those faults. The latest report dated July 30, 2015 targets the highly populated Seattle, Washington area. Are we ready for that?

If you purchase only one disaster manual for Financial Recovery and Preparedness in your lifetime, this is the ONE. For the first time ever, a FEMA inspector, a longtime expert in the disaster field, reveals what sort of help ordinary people can realistically expect from FEMA and/or their insurance company when a disaster of any type occurs.

You'll learn how to create your own disaster preparedness plan and kits but most of all, how to use Federal/State agencies and insurance companies to facilitate your own financial disaster recovery.

~Robert Winter, aka *Frecks*

INTRODUCTION

DON'T LET THIS HAPPEN TO YOU!

You can't stop a natural disaster from occurring, nor can you prevent a lot of other things from going wrong. What you can do is prepare and protect yourself and your loved ones in the years, months, weeks or even days before something transpires. Having an emergency supply kit is great, but there is so much more that you need to know in order to prevent the very worst - what I call "the disaster after the disaster" from happening when crisis actually strikes. Some of you might not have considered this or have an adequate disaster preparation plan until it is way, way too late.

After spending over 25 years working closely with disaster victims, I have found that two of the most important matters people are either not adequately informed of, or are often misinformed about, are INSURANCE and FEMA policies and procedures.

When a disaster strikes, hopefully you will have insurance and it will be the **right kind** of insurance. You will be able to call your company, they will send an adjuster to inspect your property and you'll be compensated adequately. At the same time, whether you have insurance or not, you may also need FEMA assistance. It might be extremely difficult for you to understand just how FEMA works.[2] I have witnessed many lives destroyed by this lack of information and as a result became convinced to write this book.

In my years of doing contract FEMA work, I can tell you without the least bit of doubt that disasters can hit you physically by causing injury to yourself or to family members, financially by damaging your home and your belongings, or by destroying *everything* altogether. They also often hit you mentally and emotionally by leaving you terrorized or fearful both during the disaster and the aftermath. A disaster can even hit you at such a deep level that you feel nothing but despair. You may end up thinking everything has been lost - including hope. I regularly encounter people wondering how or *if* they can ever live in their homes again. They also may be realizing at the same time that they had failed to prepare for any sort of disaster. Or, they may discover that they never actually had adequate insurance coverage although they paid high premiums faithfully thinking that they did.

It does not have to be this way! And why I'm providing you with the very valuable, even lifesaving information and advice contained in this book.

To demonstrate what I mean by "life-saving" information, let me begin with one of the main reasons I became convinced that reading this book could save not only your quality of life, but perhaps *your actual life* or the life of a loved one.

PROVIDING "HELP, HOPE, AND COMFORT"
A Hurricane Charley Story

Perhaps it was a bad omen that Hurricane Charley hit on Friday, August 13th. The first of four hurricanes to hit Florida in 2004, this Category 4 storm packed winds at 150 mph. Obviously it did a tremendous amount of destruction and caused more than 15 deaths with over $16 billion in damages. It was one of the top ten worst storms in United States history. The strength of the storm alone meant it was going to leave a lot of unhappy stories in its wake.

Here is one story from this storm:

I had been doing my inspections in post-Charley days when I ended up at a mobile home park. While finishing up my work at one home, I noticed an elderly man seated outside of his home. He looked a little worse for the wear, and so I asked him if he was okay.

In his 80's, the guy was clearly exhausted and a bit traumatized by what had just gone down in the days before. I was surprised at what had happened to his trailer as it had been clearly cut in half by the power and force of the storm. The frame sat bolted to the ground, but half of the mobile home was entirely missing.

He had a bedroom, bathroom and part of a tiny kitchen left. It was a wreck. Another inspector had already done the work, so I didn't know the full details of his losses, but he was clearly devastated. To add insult to injury, the temperatures were in the 90s and it was raining every day around 2 PM like clockwork. Not a gentle pitter patter rain, but pounding and pouring rain. Whatever wasn't ruined by the hurricane was slowly and steadily being ruined by the daily downpour and the unrepaired condition of this poor old man's home.

Sitting with him for just a few moments, I could see that he was already deeply frustrated at the lack of support he was receiving. He was definitely suffering from the elements, but an anger was building up against his insurance company. They were not responsive, and so he asked me what to do. Before I could even answer, he said, "Well, it is usually the squeaky wheel that gets the grease, so I'm gonna go ahead and keep calling and asking them to take care of my claim."

I knew that this really didn't work because most adjusters have a full case load and they look at the work in the order that it's received, not by priority and needs (including old, disabled, total losses, etc.). They also consider when the person can be contacted for an appointment. I could only give him the answer I had (and still give):

"Hey, if that doesn't work, you might want to contact a public adjuster. It is a possible 'win-win'. The more money they get you, the more money they make, plus they put pressure on the insurance company."

A public adjuster would ask for 5-50% of the gross amount of the payment - depending on state, county or federal disaster declaration. I didn't get into the details with him of whether they'd come out yet with an adjuster, etc. I just let him know that this was an option. He nodded his head, but I couldn't tell if what I said really registered with him or not.

A few weeks passed. During that time, I did other inspections in the park and made a habit of stopping by to check on him. I always had some food from the Red Cross in my vehicle and made sure he had food and water.

He was on my mind a lot though because I couldn't help but feel him very slowly but surely dying out there. There was still no funding from the insurance company, and he was literally just sitting and waiting week after miserable week.

There could be multiple explanations or reasons why this happened. Possibly he was not insured to value, or the risk was not worth the policy limit, or maybe the N.A.D.A. (National Auto Dealers Association Guides: Mobile, Modular and Manufactured Home Value Reports)[3] value was too low, or possibly the property wasn't insurable, or the risk had already been paid in a prior claim and not replaced.

Other reasons could explain his wait as well. The Red Cross facilities were packed to the rafters and there was really nowhere for him to seek better conditions. I could see how he may have started to lose all hope.

A few weeks later, he'd had enough. Without any family to vent to, with only hassles and torment from the insurance company and with the unending exposure to the weather and elements, he must have felt that he was truly at the end of his rope. He got into his vehicle, drove to his insurance company's office, went into the main lobby and shot himself in front of everyone there. He died instantly.

"At what point shall we expect the approach of danger? By what means shall we fortify against it? ...If destruction be our lot, we must ourselves be its author and finisher. As a nation of freemen, we must live through all time, or die by suicide."

~Abraham Lincoln
The Lyceum Address
January 27, 1838

SECTION ONE

IT'S YOUR RESPONSIBILITY TO HAVE FEMA AND YOUR INSURANCE COMPANY WORK FOR YOU, NOT AGAINST YOU!

MY ONGOING EDUCATION

The story I just shared with you is one reason why for most of my adult and professional life I hated everything and anything to do with insurance. I despised insurance companies, then later my opinion changed. After doing research for this book, this chapter has been aptly named because it describes just how I felt before and after. Writing this section of the book has forced me to receive a bit of enlightenment as to the truths regarding insurance companies.

WHY I HATED INSURANCE COMPANIES AND WHAT CHANGED MY MIND

I can honestly say that learning what I now know about insurance companies and insurance adjusters has definitely changed my perspective. I am not a big fan of insurance companies, but totally "get" where the adjusters are coming from, the challenges they face and the good intentions many of them have as they set out to do their jobs.

Here's my initial summary statement:

- A seasoned insurance adjuster is in a very similar situation as the experienced contract FEMA inspector. They report, "Just the facts, Ma'am", what is what, etc. They do not play favorites. They play fair.
- Insurance adjusters are only 50% of the equation where compensation is concerned. The other half of the equation is YOU - the homeowner. YOU can set the stage for a good outcome long before a disaster occurs, and YOU can do things to ensure you receive the results you want should something happen to your home.

With that being said, let's take a look at insurance and how you can protect yourself from the corporate giants and from yourself. I am going to explain all of this for you in very fine detail on the pages ahead because it is VERY important for you to know. I am also going to put it in layman's terms to the best of my ability so you can fully understand and protect yourself.

DON'T CARE, SCREW EVERYONE, AND “WHOOPS, MY BAD"

I sat down to talk with some very experienced insurance professionals in order to write this chapter and it became obvious right from the start that my years of animosity towards insurance adjusters was way off the mark. One of the first reasons that I began to take a negative view of insurance adjusters was simply because I'd watched so many contract FEMA inspectors transition from our side of the fence over to the insurance companies' side. I thought of them as betraying the disaster victims by working for the "enemy". I was making a lot of assumptions because I hadn't taken the time to learn just what it was that the adjusters actually did. I thought it was their mission or goal to go out to a property and try to get the insurance company out of any payments or as many payments as possible.

I knew of their association with my work only through the FEMA guidelines for making an application. For instance, while preparing a FEMA application, you have to provide the details of your homeowners or renter's insurance policy. At some point, you will have to fax or email the declaration page of the policy to FEMA. If or when you receive a denial letter from the insurance company, FEMA needs to get a copy of that as well. I have "sat in" on adjusters' visits to victims homes and know what sort of paperwork or assessments the adjusters did and what kind of formulas were needed, etc. What I had seen and heard was that only inexperienced adjusters were thrown out into the field when a disaster hits because the seasoned adjusters were put in offices to review claims.

I heard that many people were getting denied on their insurance claims, or that they had insufficient coverage when they had been paying for years or decades, and also that they had to wait a long time for funds. As a result, I had taken what I heard as truth and developed a dislike for insurance adjusters and insurance companies in general. Never once did I take a step back and consider if the adjusters were in similar scenarios as contract FEMA inspectors.

A QUICK COMPARISON OF INSURANCE ADJUSTERS AND FEMA INSPECTORS

The seasoned insurance adjusters are just like me - subcontractors. While working "for" a specific insurance company, they are not actually seen by that company as one of their true "team members". They are sort of outsiders, a subcontractor whose job is to scope the damage, do the paperwork and present the most accurate portrait of the "claimant" (what I call the "applicant" or the "victim"). Just like the contract FEMA inspector, the seasoned adjuster is to call it "like it is", and deal with any gray areas as accurately and honestly as possible. They are there to help out both the victim *and* the insurance company by giving the most fair, unbiased description of the entire situation.

All those years, I said that I would never be an insurance adjuster because they were only there to screw people out of money. I was wrong. It was not the adjusters who were the problem. I was shooting in the dark when I had negative thoughts about the adjusters and so I say, "my bad."

WARNING! I wasn't *completely* wrong about the insurance companies and agents though, and that is something we'll start taking a close critical look at in the coming pages.

GET REAL
The Truth About Insurance

Only a few pages ago, I shared a horrific tale from Hurricane Charley. I talked about the elderly man who gave up and killed himself at his insurance company's offices because they just wouldn't help him when he so desperately needed it. Now, let's look more closely. Were his feelings accurate? Was he right to believe that they were never coming to his rescue? That's impossible to answer, but I'm sharing this story with you in order to show you how important it is to understand all sides of the equation and how to avoid finding yourself in the same sort of condition as this man.

To be certain that you understand, I am NOT siding with anyone and providing you with some crucial information.

First, I'll provide you with the basic facts that distinguish insurance companies from FEMA. Next, I'll go over a few things about the Hurricane Charley victim's tragic story in detail. Then I will point out how you can use his heartbreaking tale in order to protect yourself more fully.

INSURANCE FACTS: A Brief Comparison

If the insurance company cannot do much for you, it is not always because they are trying to slip out of responsibility. After all, they *are* in the business to make money. Instead, it can be due to a long list of valid factors. You need to know a lot of information to be completely clear about your level of insurance protection and this is "across the board" protection - including protection from insurance companies, inexperienced adjusters and even from yourself.

You can't just buy a policy and assume that it is everything you will ever need. There is a bit of legwork required on your part, and it is more than just shopping around for a good premium. It's important that you really understand the fine print shown in your insurance policy. If you expect *replacement value* flood insurance, make sure you provide them with accurate information and that you buy the right policy that provides these things. Understand what sort of coverage you have and purchase policies that are most applicable to your particular situation.

Understand that there are different policies and a homeowners policy may not cover every situation. Consider that there is not only homeowners insurance, but also flood insurance, fire insurance, wind insurance and more. It is up to you to read the entire policy and know what is covered and what is not.

Purchase supplemental insurance if you have a lot of nice "things". I cannot begin to describe the beautiful possessions that people have lost due to a disaster and where they will never receive any compensation from their insurance company. Gorgeous Oriental rugs that are worth small fortunes would not be replaced under a homeowners policy. This should have been separately insured under a supplemental rider or plan. Other groups of valuable household items include antiques, guns, jewelry, fur coats and more.

The first thing to do is to ask your insurance provider what is going to be covered in the event of a disaster. If you keep gold coins, cash, antiques and other valuables in your home, it is likely they won't be automatically covered. For example, one of the insurance people I know said to me, "How was I to know when I sold someone the policy that their entire home was furnished in Arts and Crafts pieces? These are valuable forms of art as well as furnishings, but the homeowners policy cannot cover them." These items would have been covered *strictly* by supplemental insurance.

If you have bought and paid for a policy that will give you full replacement cost for valuables, THEN YOU CAN EXPECT THAT FROM THEM.

FEMA FACTS: A Brief Comparison

You cannot look at FEMA in the same way you view insurance companies. FEMA is NOT an insurance company.

If the insurance coverage that you have fails to stand up to your "essential needs", it is often FEMA that can provide you with access to resources. If you accept FEMA money and then the insurance comes through, you will have already signed a FEMA document stating that you will repay FEMA for whatever assistance you received if your insurance company pays for that same assistance.

You should never expect FEMA to replace your $3,000 flat screen TV that fell into flood waters. If you qualify, FEMA may award you some sort of assistance for that TV in order to meet your essential needs (see page 12), but FEMA is not the insurance company and will not give you the full replacement cost for your personal property.

Let's say you have five televisions and four were destroyed, but one still works. You would receive nothing from FEMA because the one television that works meets your essential needs. *They will give only the essentials needed to remain in your home.*

That goes for more serious matters too. For instance, if your furnace is harmed by flooding and it will cost you $4,000 for replacement, it is unlikely that FEMA is going to replace that furnace or give you that full $4,000. They may though give you some amount toward a heat source.

I stress this again: FEMA is an 'essential needs' program. You will only get *at the most* approximately $30,000 from them if you qualify and meet their criteria for eligibility. They are not insurance, they do not duplicate anything that an insurance company will pay, and they will oblige you to call your insurance company so they can also send out an adjuster. Later on, we'll discuss situations when to call FEMA and/or your insurance company.

FEMA does offer these grants that result from an inspection. FEMA also has SBA (Small Business Administration) loan programs and emergency centers called DRCs (Disaster Recovery Centers). These are available to ensure that essential needs are met, but not to help you get money for the antiques lost or on luxury items.

This is a huge distinction that many people don't understand. You have to take your share of the responsibility for knowing just what FEMA *is about* rather than just getting all upset and angry when you find out they are not going to replace everything you've lost. That is not the mission or the purpose of FEMA. If you want to be sure that you will be totally covered, that means PAYING FOR THE RIGHT INSURANCE.

KNOW WHAT FEMA CAN AND CANNOT DO

Insurance isn't the best answer, it's the only answer. Don't count on FEMA to replace all of your belongings or restore your home to pre-disaster conditions. That is never going to happen. Read the fine print. FEMA is an ESSENTIAL NEEDS PROGRAM and they can only make your home safe, secure and sanitary. If you lose everything...the dwelling, your personal property and automobile, the most you might receive is approximately $30,000. For a renter, that might be pretty good. You can pick up the pieces and move, but for a homeowner, that won't go very far.

FEMA is more of an emergency disaster funds organization to help you immediately after the storm to secure housing, food, clothing and basic essentials, especially since FEMA is there way before your insurance company with funds to get you by until your insurance provides you with some assistance. A lot of insurance companies dropped what they call *ALE* (additional living expense).[4] FEMA is there to provide that, but if you do receive assistance from your insurance or any other source for *ALE*, FEMA is going to want their money back. NO double dipping!

**WHEN IT COMES TO INSURANCE,
BE FRECKS SMART!**

Don't do like thousands of others have done in the past and try to get insurance as the hurricane is approaching landfall. Trying to get insurance at the last minute is impossible. It takes 90 days to kick in! Just ask all the want-to-be insured souls in Florida during the 2004 hurricane season where four hurricanes hit in a six-week period. No one received any insurance during that six-week period without a 90-day waiting period placed into effect.

Don't wait until that hurricane, potential flood or tornado season is upon you and try to get insurance. It's not going to happen right away.

GET THE DETAILS

Let's look more closely at some details that may explain the elderly Hurricane Charley victim's denial of benefits, his despair and ultimate suicide.

The insurance company will take the claims and assign them in the order they are received. They will assign them to an adjuster who in turn may have several claims ahead of yours. This could affect when an adjuster sees your claim. Every event is different, and so is the time it will take the provider to pay you for a claim or to even get an adjuster out to help you.

Knowing this ahead of time means you won't sit and wait fretting. Know that they will NOT usually take hasty action or rush out to "save the day!"

FEMA will try to give you what you need to remain in your home. Even then, when you do qualify for support, it can take time to get that to you because you may not have any EFTPS (Electronic Federal Tax Payment System) or another kind of electronic banking option, bank or ATM, and the postal services may be unable to hand deliver the mail. It could literally take many days or weeks.

Even when FEMA does get you support, you may still be in dire circumstances. If the insurance company cannot do much for you, it is not always going to be due to them trying to slip out of responsibility. It can be caused by a long list of valid factors.

Now, how do the details above and other additional factors such as N.A.D.A. guidelines apply to the case of the elderly man? Here are some things to consider.

Per N.A.D.A Guidelines:

a. His trailer may have been very old and not worth more than a few thousand dollars.

b. Depreciation may have caused the trailer to be worth so little that the insurance money could not even pay for repairs, let alone replacement.

c. Every case reviewed by an insurance company must be handled in the same manner as all of the others - no preferential behaviors can occur.

d. The terms of the policy may not have covered the storm or what the insurance company could provide afterward. He may not have even had coverage suitable to any sort of claim.

e. If this man did have coverage, he may have had a high deductible, and that would mean that the insurance wouldn't have kicked in.

f. He may not have had *ALE*, Additional Living Expenses (which most insurance companies have now dropped), as part of his coverage.

Other factors could have played a role in his situation. He may have been on a fixed income without the financial resources to leave his home and live elsewhere.

Impatience can also take a toll on your endurance. Try shutting off your household's electrical service on a long weekend during the hottest days of the summer. You may find that without a fridge, TV or any other conveniences, your family turns on each another. This man had been living like this for weeks on end.

And emotionally, it could simply be that he didn't have anyone to talk to and relieve his frustrations.

THE FINGER OF BLAME

It probably wasn't just one issue, namely the insurance company, that played a part in what happened to this poor, distraught man. Instead, it could have been a long list of things that he was probably unaware of which most people don't consider either. It can be all too easy to point the finger of blame. But, I'd like to remind you of the great wisdom in that old saying:

"When you point one finger of blame, you are pointing three fingers back toward **yourself**."

CAUTION! Let's not put angel wings and a halo on the insurance companies yet. Not just yet...

KNOW BEFORE YOU GO

You have to know a lot of details and be very well informed to be clear about your level of insurance protection. You need to be knowledgeable about **"across the board"** protection including protection from insurance companies, inexperienced adjusters and even protection from yourself.

Let's begin to learn how to protect yourself *from yourself*, starting with a few very accurate points.

- FACT ONE: You are not necessarily taken care of or in "sheltering arms" by your policy and there is no buddy-buddy relationship between you and your insurance company or agent. They are in the business of making money and in order to do this, they take a very specific approach to their work. This can include such things as letting you "assume" things when it may benefit them or even dropping you after a disaster hits your area.

- FACT TWO: Only three to five percent (3-5%) of the nation's insured property owners are taken care of in an ASAP manner when they make a claim. You probably guessed that it is the wealthy who never complain about their insurance situation. That's because they are taken care of almost as soon as they file a claim.

HELPFUL HINT: The wealthy probably have a second phone, business or cell phone where they can be easily reached to set up appointments whereas a person with only a home phone that is out of service from a storm or outage cannot be reached right away. Even in our high-tech world, not everyone has a cell phone. Plus, most of the wealthy have **itemized household lists** of all of their personal property which makes it very easy for an adjuster to process their claim quickly.

- FACT THREE: If you miss or skip a payment on an insurance premium and the grace period expires, you may find yourself "dropped" by that insurance company. In contrast, when you make a valid claim, you may find that same company is completely comfortable with making you wait for money or information for weeks, months or even years while they collect all of their own pertinent information. All claims should be closed ASAP, but you may even find yourself in a cycle of negotiations about figures and amounts that can take a very long time. YOU, the "insured", may have wanted something not covered or may have claimed the value of an item above the actual replacement cost. These and other factors can often delay payments.

- FACT FOUR: An insurance company may look for a loophole or example to use in order to get out of payment. For instance, if a wildfire is determined to have been due to arson and your home was burned to the ground because of it, you can be sure that the insurance company may try to get out of payments.

REMEMBER! The adjusters never behave this way. Adjusters are not trying to save the insurance company any money and only report on what's damaged, what's covered and *what the owner should receive.*

Being aware of how the above realities can help you understand the importance of taking responsibility for yourself. It's more than just shopping around for a good premium. You must accept that there is a bit of legwork required on your part, but the good news is that if you step up to the plate now, it will be a lot less likely that you find yourself at the end of your rope when a disaster does happen.

You have to see *yourself* as HALF of the problem and PART of the solution.

Let's start with a simple mathematical expression: 50/50. What this means is that the entire insurance issue can be described as: **50% of the responsibility to the insurance company, and 50% of the responsibility to the homeowner.**

The simplest illustration I can provide is this:

Insurance companies may or may not come out to do a visual inspection of a home before writing a policy. If that insurance company doesn't do the visual, they expect the homeowner to give **accurate** details and descriptions of everything from the siding to the features installed to offset risk in bad weather regions. Therefore, if your insurance company asks what sort of roof you have and you get it wrong, they may be able to decline a claim based on your inaccuracy.

Let's propose that you say you have a 'hip roof with tile', but it is actually 'a gable roof with asphalt shingles'. A hurricane occurs and causes all kinds of damage to the house. From my own construction and FEMA experience, I know firsthand that a particular roofing style can actually play a role in the amount of destruction, and that would be the case in this example.

Now the insurance adjuster pays a visit, does the inspection, notes the type of roof and has to submit an accurate report. The insurance company can now legally decline the claim because you *misrepresented* the style of roofing. Instead of a roof that was impervious to lots of weather conditions, you had one that put the house at greater risk for damage. You committed a form of fraud (in their opinion) because you also received a lower premium based on your answers and now they won't pay for the repairs.

This type of "failure" on the part of the insurance company is actually 50% YOUR fault because you didn't submit honest and accurate details.

Looking at this single example, you can see why my perspective started to shift a bit during my research after I spoke with insurance professionals at great length. I started to see that a person can't just buy a policy and assume that it's everything they'll ever need.

That means you need to learn more, begin to formulate some rules and plan ahead if you're to become and remain as protected as you need to be.

"It's your tax dollars helping people recover after a disaster. If you need help, it's your money and your right to ask for it."

~Frecks

RULES TO INSURE BY

RULE #1
Keep Your Guard Up Before, During and After a Disaster if You Want the Best Outcome

This rule means knowing what to ***expect*** as well as what you already knew. To help you, I began your education about both INSURANCE and FEMA by explaining and comparing them earlier.

Now you need to know just a little more information about FEMA before I go further. All too often I hear how victims thought FEMA was going to come in an replace everything or work in the same manner as insurance policies.

RULE #2
FEMA is Not Insurance
FEMA is an Essential Needs Program

FEMA does not work the same as insurance. You need to know in advance what it is and HOW it works. FEMA seeks the answers to the following question: *What are the **essential needs** you require to continue living in your home?* On a positive note, what I can tell you and what I've told thousands of victims is, "If FEMA gives you one dollar, it's one dollar that you didn't have before."

I'm not trying to dismiss victims and their special needs, but what I am saying is that you cannot look at FEMA to replace things covered by insurance. What if all of your belongings, even your clothing, is destroyed? For your clothing, FEMA will want to assure that you have around three full sets of clothing, but I have seen many instances where even this is gone and in need of replacement. FEMA *does* consider three sets of clothing a necessity.

This goes for more serious matters too. For instance, if your water heater is destroyed by flooding and it originally cost you $800 to replace and install, it's unlikely FEMA will replace it by giving you that full $800. But they might give you some amount towards it because you do need to have hot water.

If you do not have disaster insurance or if the insurance coverage that you do have fails to stand up to your essential needs, often times FEMA can provide you with access to resources. For example, FEMA does offer essential needs grants that result from an inspection and has SBA loan programs and emergency centers. These are all made available to ensure that your essential needs are met.

FEMA's mission and purpose is to address your essential needs only. If you want to be sure that you'll be totally covered, that means paying for insurance, which falls into the 50/50 issue. You have to take your share of the responsibility for knowing just what FEMA *is about* rather than just getting shocked, hopeless, angry or even outraged when you find out that FEMA is not going to replace everything.

RULE #3
Find Out if You Have ALE in Your Coverage

When paying for insurance, remember Rule #3: *ALE* is the "Additional Living Expenses" part of a policy that will help you by paying for housing and anything associated with your living expenses while your insurance company determines how to handle your claim.

The technical definition of *ALE* is the following:

"*Homeowners packages provide additional living expenses coverage. This will pay for some of your expenses if your home is damaged and that prevents you from living there while repairs are being made...Most policies also provide this coverage when civil authorities prohibit the use of the residence or neighborhood because of damages...*"

Typically, they will cover (above and beyond normal expenses) extra costs which may include:

- Food
- Telephone
- Housing
- Transportation to and from work and school
- Relocation
- Storage
- Utility installation
- Furniture rental for temporary residence

CAUTION: A policy may designate a limit for coverage of *ALE*, but your policy generally does not obligate the company to pay this amount up front or in full if you are suffering a partial or total loss.

In the wake of many storms, such as the four major hurricanes that hit Florida in 2004, a lot of insurance companies decided to drop the *ALE* provision altogether. This freed them from paying out the enormous sums it takes to keep people in alternative accommodations in the wake of a disaster. Any policy in effect during these storms that was eligible for *ALE* received it per storm, though each storm required a separate claim.

Just consider this: if there were four massive hurricanes again in one year and each of them left thousands of people homeless, it would mean that their *ALE* coverage would have to pay for hotel or living expenses until all the homes were rebuilt or restored. That amounted to a lot of money in the past, and though insurance companies are far from poor, it's obvious why they would have sought to avoid this.

KEEP RECEIPTS: It is up to you to keep all of the receipts that show just how much it cost you to live elsewhere while your home was being returned to a livable condition. If you do not keep track of every penny you spend, you cannot ask for every penny back from the insurance company.

ESSENTIAL NEEDS MEANS REALLY, REALLY ESSENTIAL NEEDS!

When FEMA means essential needs, it's about as bare-bones as you can get. The following are three examples of losses you might incur and the approximate amounts FEMA would likely give you as compensation. These amounts can vary from state to state or disaster to disaster.

If your $3,000 flat screen television is destroyed, FEMA more than likely will give you $75 to buy a small TV console at your nearest discounted retail chain. If your $1,500 dining room table and chairs are destroyed, FEMA may award you $45 to buy a card table and chairs. Let's say your $1,500 stereo/radio system has been ruined. You might receive $20 to go out and buy a radio.

These three very real-life examples show why you need insurance!

BE PREPARED TO WAIT: No matter how much you claim for reimbursement, you may not see it for a long time. As I stated earlier, the insurance company may take its time processing and exploring the entire claim. Normally, insurance companies in the wake of a disaster will not give an advance payment to their insureds, which is why it is sometimes advisable to get in touch with FEMA immediately after a disaster when you know you have sustained a serious loss or are forced to vacate your home.

EXAMPLE: You have a policy that includes *ALE*. A disaster hits and your home is a near total loss. You are forced to find somewhere else to live while everything is resolved. However, your insurance coverage does have the stipulation that the *ALE* is a reimbursement rather than a direct payment in advance.

What are you supposed to do?

1. You contact FEMA.
2. You file your application and include the declaration page from the homeowners policy that shows what sort of coverage you will expect. When you sign their application forms, you are also acknowledging that anything that your insurance claim duplicates in terms of assistance, you will then repay to FEMA.

3. If you qualify for assistance, you may get the temporary housing assistance you need from FEMA.

WHAT IF THERE IS NO *ALE* IN YOUR POLICY? That can go a few ways. If you have no *ALE* in your policy, this is where FEMA usually kicks in. FEMA provides hotels, mobile homes and funding assistance to people. This is only provided when there is proof that no *ALE* is going to be available and there is a limited time span that these accommodations are provided too. THIS APPLIES ONLY IF YOU QUALIFY FOR FEMA ASSISTANCE and there are many determinations and criteria for eligibility. FEMA will be discussed further in the next section.

OVER-INSURED AND UNDER-PREPARED: What about the repairs or replacement of homes? That is obviously something that has to happen after a disaster, so how does that play into the whole 50/50 rules issue? If we want to return to the example of the elderly man, we need to look at the whole over-insured issue. If that elderly man had an insurance policy that would replace his home up to $20,000, that did not mean he was going to be given that lump sum. There are a huge number of factors that an insurance company uses when assessing claims, and you can easily pay far too much insurance on a home that is not going to yield even close to the replacement amount you purchased.

Let's assume that man had a $20,000 policy but the home was worth only around $5,000 at the time. If this is the current valuation, the insurance company will only provide the actual replacement cost.

It could be worse. If the home had a market value of $5,000 but had depreciated value because of repairs or wear and tear, the formula used by the adjuster might reveal his coverage entitled him to just a few thousand or even less!

REMEMBER: The replacement cost is not always going to be the same as the amount of insurance purchased, and insurance companies don't just hand over the difference.

REPLACEMENT VERSUS ACTUAL VALUE

Now is the right moment to consider the differences between policies with replacement value and policies with actual (or depreciated) value. The following definitions are the most useful way of understanding the entire issue:

- Replacement - The amount needed to replace or repair your damaged property with materials similar to the kind and quality ***without*** deducting for depreciation (**Depreciation** means the decrease in the value of your home or personal property due to normal age, wear and tear).
- Actual Cash Value - The amount needed to replace or repair damage to your home ***after*** depreciation. For a roof that has a 20-year expectancy and now it's 17 years old? You will get only that value and not what it would actually cost for a brand new roof to be installed.

This confuses a lot of people. It usually has to do with the "bottom line". It is far less costly to insure for actual cash value, BUT IF YOU ARE IN AN AREA PRONE TO DISASTERS, IT MAY BE REMARKABLY SENSIBLE TO FORK OVER THE COST FOR A POLICY THAT WILL ACTUALLY REPLACE EVERYTHING TO THE QUALITY IT WAS AT THE VERY MOMENT THE DISASTER HIT.

Therefore, if you have a $1,500 flat screen TV and you would like it to be replaced to the same quality should something happen to it, you **DO NOT** want an actual cash value policy for the contents of the home because you will only get the exact dollar amount your insurance company has calculated for you ***after*** depreciation has been applied.

RULE #4
Determine How Much Insurance You Need in Order for Your Coverage to be Worth the Cost of the Policy

This can be hard to determine. Here's a scenario one of the insurance experts provided to me where this decision is concerned.

You have a house worth $200,000, but you buy a policy for up to one million dollars in coverage. Then, disaster strikes and your home is totaled, leveled and gone. The insurance company, right from the start, looks at the value of the home as only $200,000 and depreciates it from 10 to 20 percent. They give you that amount of money to begin rebuilding.

As you get close to the end of the process, they reassess the issue and give you what is actually needed. Although you paid a much higher premium per year, the final amount of money you receive will still not be the difference between the first amount and the one million dollars you had been paying for.

This financial reality is because the insurance company is working with **actual values** and not the numbers insured for in the policies. It is all about replacement - not about the amount of insurance you purchased. Thus, many people are floored to learn that they are not getting the cash difference between the replacement value of the home and the size of the policy they had been paying for. Whatever it **ACTUALLY** costs to rebuild is what you are going to get.

In these situations, there is usually also personal property to consider. The adjusters have to work with the owners to understand what they ACTUALLY had in the home. There are many worksheets designed to streamline this process (see pages 113-121), but insurance is still a system open to failure. It doesn't cover everything in a home and an inexperienced adjuster may overlook things, fail to get the figures right, etc.

CAUTION: This tells us that we have to do things like household inventories and thoroughly read our policies to know what is covered and to what extent.

RULE #5
Understand Exactly What You are Paying For

Understand what sort of coverage you have and purchase policies that are the most applicable to your particular situation. Understand that there are different insurance policies and that a homeowners policy may not cover **every** situation. For instance, there is homeowners insurance, but there is also flood insurance, fire insurance, wind insurance and more. The elderly man in the story I shared may not have had any coverage for a hurricane, flood or wind. He may have kept a policy with only fire insurance.

REMEMBER: We DO KNOW he had insurance because his final act was against the insurance company. However, his distress may have actually been due to the fact that his insurance company could offer him no support because he did not have the CORRECT coverage. He may have been paying for the lowest level of insurance possible because of his fixed income. That investment may have been a waste of his money because it wasn't providing him with much protection at all. He also may have opted for high deductibles in order to get lower premiums and that too can work against a victim or claimant. Finally, he may have had a policy but failed to realize that there was no *ALE* provision in it.

I saw this type of confusion about what was covered and what was not

> **WARNING!**
>
> In ALL flood insurance policies, there is NOT AN *ALE* ALLOWANCE. You are told this by the insurance agent and often asked to sign a document indicating that you are aware of this lack of coverage and that you understand everything about your flood insurance policy. Many people appear to have forgotten this transpired when they first purchased their plans!

when I was working the Hurricane Sandy disaster in New York and New Jersey. People said to me, "I've had this policy for 40 years and never knew that I was not covered AND my insurance company never told me!" I've heard this same thing for 25 years, but it was tenfold in a situation like Hurricane Sandy because hardly anyone was carrying flood insurance!

Why did this happen? Most of the time, the people had phoned their insurance company in order to begin filing a claim. The insurance company would respond that the damages were due to flooding, and that the homeowner did not have a flood insurance policy. Then, the claimant would argue and say it was a hurricane that caused the damages, but the insurance companies would point out that it was flooding that had caused the damages. The insurance company would send out adjusters and then issue a "No Claim".

This battle of semantics would put the homeowners in a real pickle. They thought they'd had coverage but ended up without any. They had not read their policies thoroughly enough to see that it would have required a flood insurance policy. PLUS, their insurance company had never indicated to them that they were paying for a plan that offered them nothing - no compensation at all if there ever was a hurricane where damage resulted in flooding.

A lot of people may call me cynical for pointing out that this particular area of New York and New Jersey was at sea level (or barely above) and that loads of homes and buildings were in sight of the ocean! Why these homeowners did not pursue flood insurance is a mystery to me. Yes, they had not experienced any sort of serious hurricane or flooding for decades, but still...

Regardless, most of these disaster victims were still shocked to learn that the policies they'd been happily paying for years were only providing them with partial coverage at best, regardless of any deductibles.

RULE #6
Think About What it is Truly Going to "Cost" You if There is a Disaster

Few of us understand the diverse realm of possibilities that can transpire after a disaster. We may experience wind damage, wildfire damage, earthquake damage plus even more unexpected happenings. Despite what we cannot predict and though we may not be able to anticipate just what might happen to our homes, most of us DO understand our own personal financial capabilities. We know if we can fund only a few thousand dollars in repairs "out of pocket" or if we cannot.

With that in mind, you need to anticipate what sort of insurance coverage you should choose.

Everyone wants a **lower premium** and can get this in several ways. For example, you might have a home equipped with the best construction materials and household systems that cause your insurance premiums to be reduced due to the safety in the home's design. In this case, you might choose to pay a lower premium while accepting a higher deductible.

This would mean that you would only put in an insurance claim when a hefty amount of damage had been done and a large amount of money is going to be required for repairs or replacement. Or, you might opt for the reverse and pay for a much **more expensive premium** that retains a very low deductible. This would allow you to make calls for repairs that cost you a very small amount of money out-of-pocket if a disaster occurs.

Obviously, these choices are something entirely up to the owner depending on their available budget and needs, but what does it all mean when there is actually a disaster?

It means that you need to consider what is realistic for you to be paying for monthly premiums **BEFORE** that future disaster happens. It also means you need to figure out just how much out-of-pocket outlay would be reasonable for your budget AFTER an event happens.

Let's say you might choose a higher deductible, such as a $5,000 deductible. As a result, when a disaster hits, you would only get in touch with your insurance provider once you know with absolute certainty that more than $5,000 in damage has occurred. In fact, the general "rule of thumb" is to only call when you are sure that there has been around two to three times the amount of the deductible property damage done.

Why that much? Because it guarantees that you will not get what is called a "No Claim" letter, the official letter from the insurance provider indicating that you will not be getting money to handle repairs. Doing this also puts you on the insurance company's "radar" so to speak, and that is something that can put you at risk for being dropped or having premiums jacked up so high that you would soon drop the provider yourself.

NOTE: Traditionally, homeowners premiums can only be raised if there has been a net loss to the insurance company in that region in recent consecutive years.

This is something we already looked at above, but is another reason to give your coverage a lot of thought ahead of time.

I also need to emphasize another major point: IF you apply for any sort of FEMA assistance, you will be required to get in touch with your insurance company. That means that you need to make an insurance claim if you're going to follow up and request any assistance through FEMA.

This can also prove problematic to a lot of people. After all, some people may have decided to forgo their insurance companies because they have high deductibles. They may already know they won't qualify for any monetary claims because they don't have that amount in damages.

Yet, at the same time, they may need support from FEMA for essential needs in the days or weeks after the storm. They may want to also see if FEMA assistance is available to them for any of the repairs.

FEMA will require you to present the "denial" letter sent by the insurance company - a denial of coverage or proof of what is covered from the insurance provider. Remember, FEMA doesn't want to double up and pay you a second time for something the insurance company is already handling.

After contacting your insurer, there is also the risk we just mentioned above: a claim into the insurance company is going to draw their attention to you. You could now be on their radar in terms of your home being in a disaster zone. This could lead to a spike in the price of your premium or, I have seen people dropped altogether because of the risks of further storms and damages.

WARNING: You may be told by your insurer that this is not the case.

Over the years, I've also seen a lot of disaster victims fall for what seems to me like an insurance company "acting script" when they encourage disaster victims to contact FEMA because they can't help them. Instead of being really honest and saying they can't help you, they refer you.

I call this the *Buddy Act*, an attitude that proves to me that they are no one's buddy, pal or good neighbor, and plainly looking out for their own bottom line. This "valuable" FEMA information is the *same* information FEMA makes available to all on television, radio, newspapers, on posters and everywhere else they can after a disaster occurs.

On the other hand, there is also the fact that the person buying the insurance *should really have known what their policy would cover.* Sure, shame on the insurance company for taking monthly premium dollars from you then passing the buck to FEMA, but even more shame on the homeowner who doesn't read their own insurance policy to understand its coverage and limitations. Again - one finger forward, three fingers back.

You really need to think things through in advance! You need to consider the full spectrum of your financial capabilities BEFORE choosing your insurance coverage.

Start with the deductibles and be realistic about the amount of money you would have *on hand* to make repairs after a disaster. What could you realistically afford to handle on your own, and how much is the actual cutoff point before you would need help?

It might be pretty tough to understand all of this. For instance, when do you actually call FEMA and when do you hold off? When is it wise to put in an insurance claim and when isn't it so smart?

Let me offer you my own table of decision-making rules. Be **FRECKS SMART** and know the chart shown on the following page.

This might seem too simple at first, so to explain this table further, find out IF you are eligible for assistance per FEMA's criteria.

The last row of this chart is the most important. Really consider what's in front of you and what the consequences might be if you do or do not make that call.

FRECKS' TABLE

Incident	Renter	Owner
Catastrophic Damage	Call FEMA and insurance.	Call FEMA and insurance.
No Insurance	Call FEMA.	Call FEMA.
Moderate Damage (50% loss - usually two to three times your deductible)	Call FEMA and call the insurance company.	Call FEMA and call the insurance company.
Damage twice as much as deductible or less	Think about it...review all of the information above.	Think about it...review all of the information above.

You should now have enough information to really understand the chain of events that go on after a disaster and how your budget has to figure into the equation.

DUE DILIGENCE
More About Insurance Split Coverage and Limitations

The insurance companies do actually review each policy prior to renewal, although they do it to find ways to bump up prices or to make sure that insured items are in the same condition they were in the previous year.

As an example, an insurance company rarely issues a homeowners policy without doing at least a "drive by" of the property to be covered (or in today's world, a Google Earth shot of the property). They might see that a fence is needed along a retaining wall or that something is not as described by the person buying the insurance. They might even do a full-blown inspection. The point is they don't just walk blindly into the situation and leave themselves open to risk. Someone in the firm does the due diligence to make sure that things are "status quo" and that no major problems seem to appear.

If the insurance companies do that, why don't homeowners do the same and exercise due diligence for their own benefit? Why do they just walk relatively blind into their coverage and make all kinds of assumptions about what is going to happen in the event of a disaster or other event? I don't really know the answer to that question. What I CAN tell you is what I have seen consistently: homeowners who are utterly astonished that they DON'T have coverage.

I can only wonder what these people were thinking when they kept sending in their checks. Why did they pay for something when they didn't take the time to determine just what it provided? Did they even look at their policies?

WARNING! Does doing this guarantee that you can always have coverage? The answer is NO.

AN INSURANCE STORY

Before going much further in this section, I want to share an important illustration of the points we will continue to touch on throughout the rest of this section.

The story goes like this:

A few years ago, there were some major fires in California. This began with the work of an arsonist. This imbecile set fires that were then quickly spread by the seasonal Santa Ana winds. The winds picked up the embers and debris, eventually causing out of control fires from the Los Angeles area all of the way down into San Diego County.

Many people suffered losses due to the fires. As the homeowners began to submit their claims, it became clear that a few insurance companies had decided to refuse making payments by saying that the policyholders did not have any coverage. Why? Because the fires were the result of arson.

Their logic was deeply flawed and they ended up looking like greedy fools. Had each of the homeowners gone and set their homes on fire, then yes, they could have most certainly denied the claims. However, the arson that caused the homes to burn was not an intentional act on the parts of the owners, and so the claims had to be paid.

At the time, they were using software programs that would give a sort of ballpark figure as to the cost of the repairs, replacement, etc. Several of the insurance companies liked this process. However, many owners opted to do a bit of legwork on their own and get three bids for rebuilding their homes. Clearly, the three-bid process would be much more accurate. And again, it became yet another issue of the replacement cost.

Remember that poor man in the trailer park we discussed at the opening of this book? He may have been offered money (we'll never know), but it may have been so little that it seemed like a joke. This may have been due to replacement costs gauged by the insurance company using a program that spat out a figure based on some basic details. This same thing began to occur in the California fires and people who had insured their homes for $500,000 might be offered only $200,000 because that is what these programs said would "replace" all that had been lost.

Thus, the old "over insured" dilemma rears its ugly head again. These people had paid for a lot of insurance thinking it would kick in and help them rebuild no matter what, but they didn't really read the terms in the policy. The insurance company can do some sort of formal calculations and try to prove that it had indeed been fair and accurate, but it could still be far, far off the mark. You may be able to receive only a portion of what you thought you could because you paid too much for insurance.

Interestingly enough, a lot of people in this particular incident decided to dicker with the insurance companies. Some spent almost two years in tents in their front yards going back and forth with the insurance firms until they got what they felt was realistic, or until one or both parties simply burned out and settled for whatever they could.

In other words, the insurance companies may let people pay for too much coverage, and even then they try to wear people down with all of the "to and fro" when a valid claim is submitted. You might know that you should get $300k to rebuild and replace, but they offer $175k. You then say you want that $300k. They come back a few weeks later with a revised offer of $208k, and you hold firm. This can go on for months or years...and it has!

Adjusters do try to work with you, and the claim remains open until the homeowner eventually settles. It can end up being a matter of "when" rather than how much.

As I say now, I can't hate all insurance companies. I thought before that they deliberately tried to screw people out of their money, but they do hire adjusters who don't technically work for them. Adjusters are neutral and report the facts.

And it isn't all black and white. A lot of gray areas stand in between.

INSURANCE COMPANY PATTERNS
The Big Picture

I want to emphasize some facts again. I pointed out that you have to look at your biggest risks as individual issues and purchase separate coverage for most of them. Consider that you might have a really good homeowners insurance plan, but there is not likely going to be fire, flood, wind or other extreme coverage. There is also not likely going to be replacement coverage for things like fur coats, jewelry, antiques and/or art either. Think of the homeowners policy as a sort of foundation on which you have to build up the rest of the coverage. Also, just because you had coverage for many years doesn't mean that your insurance firm is going to just keep on renewing that plan.

As an illustration, look for a moment at life insurance coverage. Usually when you buy "term" insurance, it is cheaper when you are young and then it goes up in price every year. As you get older, the cost of the insurance can be quite nutty. I've seen policies where an 80+ year old buyer might have to shell out tens of thousands for a year of coverage. There is a limit to coverage, and life insurance policies do tend to become unavailable after a certain age because the risk is too high for the insurance company. Offer a policy to someone almost 100 years old and it's more than likely you'll be paying out on it in the very near future!

The companies that offer insurance coverage for floods, fires, storms, etc. have this same mindset. If there hasn't been a disaster in an area for decades and then the region experiences one, it is likely that the insurance companies will continue to offer the plans. They might increase costs to recover their so-called "losses" that came from paying claims, but that might be the extent of it. However, if disasters in an area continue to strike, such as what happened to New York and New Jersey following Hurricanes Irene and Sandy, it can be entirely possible that an insurance company will drop clients, increase prices to such an extent that people drop them, or even stop extending policies of a certain kind. In other words, I have seen instances where everyone who applied and got a No Claim or denial letter was subsequently dumped by the company or had their rates increased so much that they could not afford the coverage and canceled it themselves.

Ugly certainly, but true. I have also seen another facet of insurance - individuals who do pay the hefty policy prices and are usually the folks who are dealt with first. For example, in an area I have responded to with FEMA where both rich and poor experienced losses due to a disaster, the wealthy policyholders got their needs met immediately by their insurance providers. After all, these are the people who were paying out enormous sums every year to get full and complete coverage of all kinds.

It is simple economics. Does it pay for the insurance company to give a lot of attention to the homeowner with a $25,000 policy or the one with the $2 million plan? Clearly, insurance is a business, and because of that, it boils down to the largest revenue stream getting the most dedication and attention.

WARNING: Insurance companies will tell you that this is not true.

The good news is that the best seasoned adjusters don't take any of this into consideration. When a disaster hits and they are called out to assess properties, they tend to always use the "first in, first out" rule. You could be Johnny Millionaire, yet you might wait for the seasoned adjuster to handle the 50 to 500 poor or working class people who may have called in ahead of you. Fair is fair in the world of insurance adjusters, so the whole financial component is not going to factor into how you are handled when a disaster strikes and the adjusters are in control.

Now, does that mean that I might have given that elderly man who became so frustrated that he committed suicide the wrong advice? Should I have actually encouraged him to be a squeaky wheel and pester the insurance company?

After speaking with seasoned adjusters, the general consensus among them was **no.** Here's why. The *squeaky wheel gets the grease* gambit will work with about half of the adjusters in the field. You might pester one adjuster into heading to your home ahead of others. You might call every day and just drive that adjuster nuts enough to respond to get you off their back. However, you may also run the risk of bothering that adjuster so much that they make a point of putting you at the very bottom of the list. You might also annoy a seasoned adjuster who just takes your call and continues to tell you that they'll get to you when it's your turn. You can never know what will happen if you beg them to hurry up and come over to your place.

You **CAN** know with absolute certainty that most seasoned adjusters are not easily influenced in either direction.

Sounds a bit like the work I do as a FEMA Inspector. If you have already read the incredible disaster stories from my book, *Dust in the Wind*, this situation goes down memory lane.

ADJUSTERS AND INSPECTORS
A Second Look

Because one of the goals of this book is to help readers understand how to get the best outcome after a disaster, I want to elaborate further about the comparison between seasoned FEMA inspectors and seasoned insurance adjusters. I already noted some of the similarities and differences at the beginning of this book, but there are more "insider" details you should be aware of. The two are a lot more alike in some ways than I'd ever realized before.

Consider:

- We both have to deal with calls as they come and we should not be using any preferential treatments or behaviors.
- We cannot be influenced by anything that a homeowner says or does.
- We cannot take gratuities or offers of anything from the victims.
- We both have to "tell it like it is" and try our best to clarify any gray areas with the utmost fairness and accuracy.
- Neither of us determines what, IF ANY, returns are gained by filing the application or making a claim.
- Inexperienced adjusters on both sides tend to make similar mistakes while the seasoned experts can go in and get the job done without any undo influences or errors in judgment.
- In both groups, when a disaster strikes, it is not uncommon for the best or the most seasoned adjusters and inspectors to become "desk bound" or to be put to work doing "on the fly" training. Where insurance adjusters are concerned, the very best and most seasoned are often kept at headquarters where they review documentation before it is forwarded to the main office. This means that a huge number of inexperienced adjuster or inspector mistakes are made while the top dogs are stuck back at the office on large disasters until the workload slows down.
- There are good and bad in both groups, and some (in fact, it is more accurate to say MANY) adjusters and inspectors may have a lot of experience with only one kind of disaster until they get sent out for

another.

This means an adjuster may have a lot of flood experience and so too may the FEMA inspector, but then a tornado strikes and both of them may be handling such an incident for the first time as they tackle their work in the field.

Of course, that last factor also shows a major difference between them. For the most part, the seasoned contract FEMA inspector will have a long list of disaster "types" under his or her belt. He responds all over the United States and in U.S. territories. In comparison, a seasoned insurance adjuster may not have such an extensive background and find that they don't encounter much outside of homeowners policies and maybe a few flood policies until a really big disaster hits.

Are they identical, apart from that one issue? No, there are a lot of other differences too. Where a FEMA inspector and an Insurance adjuster really differ is in their level of involvement.

NOTE: In 2015, FEMA changed the name of inspectors from Contract FEMA Inspector (CFI) to Disaster Assistance Employee (DAE). For the purposes of this manual, CFI or FEMA inspector will still be used.

Here is what I mean:

- The contract FEMA inspector has some basic issues assessing, verifying and reporting damages so that FEMA can make a determination on specific assistance. For example, let's say that all of the clothing in a home is destroyed or left in unusable condition. The FEMA inspector indicates this to be the case and then FEMA determines what, if any, assistance is given to that household based on the facts. The way that this assessing, verifying and reporting is done is very simple. The inspector has to indicate one of three types of damage on the report. He or she is essentially out there to verify damages and to what type of property. To illustrate this point, is it personal property or real property? What is it? How was it damaged? This is a process that really slows down an inspection because it requires three facts to be listed for everything that is damaged. Here's an example: I go to a home to do the inspection. I see that a refrigerator is damaged by the disaster. I have to indicate three things: "I saw it and verified it", "I didn't see it but there were damages to property indicative of the loss ", or "I didn't see it but damages were not sufficient to prove loss." I also have to explain how the damages were done (flood, wind, earthquake, wind-driven rain).
- In contrast, the insurance adjuster handles things such as actual pricing. They might have to use a computer program that requires things like the square footage of a home in order to gauge the amount

due to the homeowner. They also have to determine the level of loss. Was the house a total loss? What dollar amount of damage has been done, etc.? The insurance adjuster has a lot more gray areas to deal with and a lot more "fine detail" information to handle.

- The insurance side of things requires a great deal more information. For example, there are programs that can be used to figure out just how much of a loss was sustained, unless the home contains 'above average' contents. The programs might feature worksheets for each room and ask such things as, "Was there a TV?" or "Was there a single sofa?" It is then part of the adjuster's task to calculate the values of such things. If you say you had a bric-a-brac collection in a specialized cabinet, that might cause a delay in your claim while the adjuster attempts to determine the value and other factors.
- FEMA inspectors don't deal with these things as we are an "essential needs" program and not an insurance firm.
- While a lot of the contract FEMA inspectors use a preliminary review prior to the submission of an inspection in order to avoid any inspections being returned, insurance adjusters may not have this same system in place. Delays in claims can happen for this very reason. An inexperienced adjuster may do the paperwork incorrectly, send it to the main offices and get it back with a demand for corrections. This can happen when an adjuster is handling a massive case overload all due to inexperience with the paperwork and they might get that same case back over and over again.
- You will only see the FEMA inspector once for approximately 30 minutes, whereas the insurance adjuster may come back to the property several times before your claim is finished and you sign on the dotted line.

As you can see, all of these factors can add up to some serious threats to the homeowner who is hoping for the fairest, most timely and straightforward experience. There are a lot of variables that can impact the outcome of their claim or visit by an insurance adjuster or a contract FEMA inspector.

Because we are going to do an entire section on the steps for a good FEMA inspection in Section Two, I won't go over how to handle a FEMA inspection just yet. I do want to help you learn more now about exactly how to protect yourself where the entire insurance company issue as well as their visit is concerned.

REMEMBER: The title of this section is how to protect yourself from the insurance companies and from yourself. You will hear again and again that you still have a very substantial role to play in all of this. You now know many different things that may affect how you recover from a disaster, but the key factor that I haven't yet touched upon in depth yet is "Your Own Part" in actually protecting yourself.

THE MOST OVERLOOKED ITEMS ON INSURANCE CLAIMS

Make sure to include all inventory lost on your insurance claim. This includes all of the food and other perishables in your kitchen refrigerator/freezer, your garage freezer (if applicable) or any other location you stored perishable food that was lost due to damage.

Bathroom items such as paper products, soaps, etc. - even medicines stored in your bathroom cabinets, can easily add up to an additional $500 to $2,500 or more and can be added to your claim.

HOW DO YOU PROTECT YOURSELF?

I was speaking with a very seasoned insurance adjuster who had actually once also worked as a contract FEMA inspector. He later switched teams and started working as a contract storm adjuster for the insurance companies. What he said to me during one of our conversations while I was writing this book was this:

"Let's say you're someone getting a knee replacement. If you ask your physician, he or she will say that their part of the job is around 20% and that the other 80% is up to you. The percentage that is your responsibility involves you doing the work, exercises, therapy and keeping a positive attitude. So, people filing insurance claims have to understand that they have to do their part too. It is actually a give and take - more of a 50/50 venture with insurance, but they still have to do their part."

I asked him what it is that a homeowner has to do. He went on to say that they need to make sure they are covered correctly long before anything happens, and to then “do the right thing” once something does occur.

“So, what is the right thing?” I asked. From his perspective, I wanted to know.

"Well," he said smiling, "you've got to grill ‘em. "

I wasn't exactly sure what he meant.

He gave these examples:

- *How long have you done this?*
- *Do you handle floods?*
- *Do you handle hurricanes?*
- *What is your background?*
- *Do you handle all of these situations or just one?*
- *What insurances do you handle? Wind? Flood? Fire?*

Ask all of the above when an inspector/adjuster arrives at your home. Be as direct as you can and put the emphasis on learning just how much experience this person might have in your type of issue. It is entirely fair and legal to grill them in this way because you **DO** have the right to challenge the outcome, and if you know you've been sent an inexperienced adjuster who has very little history with your type of disaster, you may not get a fair and accurate insurance claim.

With total honesty, in all of my years doing contract FEMA inspections, I never felt bad or reacted poorly to someone asking me how long I had done this job. Even when they have a lot of doubt in their voice as they pose a question, I don't feel offended. I'm glad to explain my level of experience and reassure them that they are in trustworthy hands.

I also tend to encourage them to ask me anything they need to know while they have me at the site. After all, the chance to ask all kinds of FEMA-related questions is probably not going to come up easily again for the victim.

If an insurance adjuster or FEMA Inspector gets all testy over a few questions, it's a good indicator that you should heavily scrutinize the outcome of their work and ask to double-check what they do.

With all of that being said, there is a difference between just asking questions or being distracting. While I do encourage people to ask me questions and a good insurance adjuster might do the same, if you do ask continual questions and generally distract us from our work, it is quite likely that we will miss something important, and that means YOU lose. Ask your questions and then let that person do their job.

You can also protect yourself *from yourself* by allowing an adjuster or inspector to do their work without a lot of unnecessary disruptions. If you have quarreling kids in the house, a loud TV or stereo blasting, a lot of people hanging around or anything else that could cause an adjuster or inspector to be distracted, it's your possible loss. They might miss some damage or an issue that should have been documented.

That brings us to the point where you learn just what the insurance adjuster feels you should receive. You may find that you disagree with some part or even all of his or her findings.

NOTE: If a FEMA inspector is at your home, you will be told that FEMA will contact you within 7 to 10 days to inform you of your assistance.

Are you done? No! There are a few more steps you can now take after the inspection and make decisions in order to protect yourself further, fight for yourself and your family and get the most accurate offer.

FIGHTING THE BIG GUYS
Responding to the Insurance Company

In a perfect world, you would live through a disaster, see that your home incurred damages, have adequate insurance to cover all repairs and renovations, then get a seasoned adjuster to come out to assess the level of damage. The adjuster would then report it all correctly and fairly to your insurance company. Then you would get the money you need in order to get your home back to normal.

Obviously, we don't live in a perfect world, and my own experience and that of others has shown that there can be all kinds of glitches in the process I've just described, such as:

- You might have the insurance needed, but you might not get a seasoned adjuster.
- You might get that seasoned adjuster, but distract them or cause them to report something inaccurately.
- You might decide to be a squeaky wheel and force the adjuster to come out under a dark cloud of aggravation and annoyance with you.
- You may not agree with what the adjuster determined or the amount the insurance company wants to pay.

The list can go on and on. So what's a beleaguered homeowner to do? Using some examples of possible circumstances, here are a few effective ways you can respond!

DISPUTE SCOPE OF LOSS

You get your report or details from the adjuster and see that they are not compensating you for the refrigerator in the basement. This is a time for a "dispute scope of loss" claim.

The adjuster comes out and inspects your property. You then get an offer for repairs. If you pretty much agree with everything that is said but find you have a problem or issue with one or two minor points about the offer made, you can **dispute the scope of loss**.

If this happens to you, just call the insurance company and ask for another adjuster or supervisor. Indicate that you disagree with the assessment and take a minute to explain why. This remedy often falls into the category of "best case scenario" and is nothing to cry about if you find yourself actually making such a call.

Most insurance companies expect this sort of minor stuff and may go back and forth with you on some points, but generally such things are resolved without a lot of headaches and hair pulling.

APPRAISAL

You get the offer from the insurance company and it's trying to settle the claim at roughly $100,000 less than the monetary amount you know you need to rebuild. This is a time to consider an appraisal.

If you feel that you need to dispute the claim on a much larger basis and not just a few small issues that would be easy to handle with a dispute on the scope of loss described above, then you need to request **the appraisal**. This involves what is known as an "intermediary" (and there can actually be several of them), and then at least two appraisers (there can be several more of these as well). What are these folks assigned to do? How does an appraisal work? This situation is not something that the insurance company really wants to see happen because the insured is often angry if they lose. The insurance company wins the majority of these appraisals unless there is something missing or incorrect in the estimate.

Example: Let's say that your home burned to the ground and the insurance company is persistently offering you a sum that is inadequate for your needs to rebuild. To make sure of this, you went out and got three different bids and all prove that the insurance company's figure is off the mark. You got the bids from local contractors that guarantee accuracy. You show the insurance company this information, and yet they might still say that their own figures are fair and accurate.

That's when you whip out the appraisal card. They really don't want to go there because they know there's a chance they will lose. They may begin upping their offer by measurable increments to keep you from actually calling the Insurance Commissioner and beginning that process (described in the next paragraph). This is not the time to cave in because your bids will have proven that you are due a much larger amount. Go ahead and ask for those intermediaries and appraisers now. They will work to determine the realistic sum and then a ruling will come down. How often does the insurance company lose in such cases? Roughly 25% of those cases go to the homeowner and not the insurance company simply because the evidence usually points to the insurance company as being the accurate one. While you may not get all of the money you want, you may get a decision that is more favorable.

COMPLAINT TO THE INSURANCE COMMISSIONER

The adjuster came out, behaved very erratically and the insurance company is not responding to the horrible assessment that the adjuster did. Instead, they are sticking to the adjuster's report as if it is fact and ignoring your concerns and your request for a new adjuster.

When an insurance company is not responsive and you feel that you have a valid concern, you can file a formal complaint with the insurance commissioner in your area. However, you should know that when you take things to this level, everyone involved is investigated. That means that you are investigated just as intensely as the insurance company and the adjuster who handled the claim.

Additionally, the commissioner takes these matters seriously. When you make the call, there is usually an investigator at your home or business the very next day. Insurance companies really don't want to go there either. It would force them to open their books without any sort of reservation to the person in charge of the complaint, which is not usually something the insurance company is comfortable doing. It's not because they regularly conceal things, but rather that every little detail is thoroughly scrutinized and even a tiny error on their part will be quickly uncovered and heavily penalized. At the same time, it's not the very worst nightmare you can create to get the insurance company to behave fairly.

BAD FAITH

You call to file a claim and when the adjuster comes out, they indicate they don't believe you sustained the damage indicated. You might have repaired a roof because of a hurricane, but the adjuster did not come for a week or two and did not see the original damage. They may wrongly say you did not have damage. Are they acting in "Bad Faith"?

Those two words are a nightmare to most insurance companies. That's because ***bad faith*** means that the insurance company is actually behaving in a fraudulent manner. Essentially what this claim means is that you have damage, that an insurance adjuster says that you have no damage and the insurance company is backing their claim. There are a lot of ways this can pan out.

Consider these examples:

- You might have had a horrible wind storm that actually lifted the roof slightly off the home. This pulled up nails and caused loads of leaks. The adjuster came out, saw it and said, "No, this isn't damage. It's deferred maintenance." The insurance company holds to the adjusters claim and won't pay as promised.
- You have a hurricane that pulls some siding and a lot of roofing off the home. Because there are daily rains and more winds, you pay for the repairs and wait for the adjuster to arrive. He or she comes out many days or weeks later, sees that all is well and refuses to accept your claim. The insurance company holds to this, and even when you show that you have receipts for the work and/or materials, this would be investigated by the insurance company.

One man I spoke to had a really amazing story about bad faith. He received a letter from the insurance company he had used for more than 20 years where they told him they were dropping him as a customer because his roof was "curling". This guy was a knowledgeable building contractor and yet he had absolutely no idea what that term even meant. He asked around and found that no one he knew had ever heard of it either, nor had anyone ever been dropped by an insurance provider because of it. Even worse was the fact that every year he had faithfully climbed up on the heavy, wooden shake roof and done whatever maintenance was needed.

So, what was the deal? The company did an annual review and probably saw that this property was of a certain age. When they did some sort of preliminary drive by or visual inspection (can we say Google Earth?), they didn't like the look of the roof. They created this bizarre “curling” term and sent the letter. Rather than just accepting this nonsense, the man sent a letter indicating he was about to bring a suit against the firm for "bad faith". Any act on the part of the adjuster and insurance company to deny coverage or a claim can prompt the owner to file the bad faith claim.

Clearly, that changed their tune and they offered to extend his coverage. Despite their effort, their actions had opened the man's eyes to the low quality of the firm so he shopped around and found a reputable company with a more dependable plan.

IF you speak the words *bad faith* to an insurance agent or company, you are usually going to see an immediate reaction. This is because they understand you are not messing around. In fact, most insurance companies know that very few consumers are even aware of this or any of the other options I have presented above for you to use.

To hear someone say they are going to hang up the phone and place a call to the insurance commissioner to file a claim of bad faith is like a "Code Red" full alert issue for an insurance provider. Not only are they likely to lose that sort of case, but they could be heavily penalized for behaving in such an irresponsible manner. The person who files the valid claim (and you had better be sure it is valid before you go for it!) is often given from two to ten times the amount they were initially due. This is purely punitive to the insurance company, but also an attempt at compensation for the claimant’s hardship, loss and suffering. If your insurance company refuses to pay out a claim that was reasonably worth, for example, $100,000, a court can actually demand that you receive $1 million instead.

WARNING! Be sure your claim is valid. If you are wrong, misrepresent anything or lose, you could end up paying for all the costs of the suit.

NOW THAT YOU KNOW

You now know what a lot of people never discover: that the insurance firms do not own you outright. They can use less then efficient tactics in the days and weeks after a disaster hits such as sending out inexperienced adjusters, but they will generally pay what the covered loss is and it's always that 50/50 issue. When you take the time to read your insurance policy and really understand what is covered, you are part way through the battle. When you also take the time to figure out your legal options for recourse against an adjuster's findings or an insurance company's response, you are even further along the path to success.

But, now there is one more major thing you need to know in order to completely protect yourself...

THE #1 THING THEY DON'T WANT TO HEAR

Naturally, I am on the scene at several points in the disaster recovery process. I have even been involved long after people have dealt with their insurance adjusters, the back and forth that goes on over claims and all the rest. What I have learned after all these years is that there are two MORE words that no insurance adjuster or insurance company ever wants to hear: Public Adjuster.

PUBLIC ADJUSTER

You might be scratching your head now saying something like, "Isn't that other person who came here an adjuster too?"

The answer is yes, but to be certain that you really understand things, let's take a quick look at the three kinds of adjusters:

1. Company Adjuster - This is the adjuster who works FOR the insurance company. More than likely this is someone who may not be out in the field but who is going to review all of the claims. There can be in-house company adjusters in the field too, but they will be in the field less often than a subcontracted storm adjuster.
2. Independent Adjuster - Usually these are people employed by an independent adjusting firm contracted by the insurance companies to handle claims. Because few insurance companies have enough in-house adjusters to handle claims, they work with larger firms offering contract adjusters. This means that the independent adjuster is NOT working FOR the insurance company. As I emphasized earlier, they have no bias that would seek to create favorable conditions for the insurance firm. Don't feel threatened by the independent adjuster since they are just like the contract FEMA contractors. They are not part of the larger entity. They are fair because that is their job.
3. Public Adjuster - These are adjusters who do not work for the insurance companies or the independent adjustment firm. More than likely, they were once an employee of one or the other but have now gone entirely independent and work only FOR YOU and for themselves specifically. They contract with policyholders to help them settle claims with the insurance company. They are given the right to negotiate and agree upon a figure that is acceptable to both parties, and they are rewarded with a percentage of the settlement. The fees that public adjusters quote are not set by state or federal guidelines. A homeowner must contact the county or city to find out the legal amount the public adjuster can ask for and receive.

Knowing about the amount a public adjuster can receive is something that is also part of that "50/50" responsibility issue. Why? During the 2004 hurricane season, an emergency order was created to place a cap on the amount public adjusters could charge.

Their profits had been so substantial that the emergency order set the maximum dollar amount at 10 percent.

THE THREAT

Now you know about all three "players" and it's time to discover why it is that public adjusters are the most threatening to insurance companies. Why do insurance firms dislike public adjusters so much? If you pick up a newspaper in an area where a major disaster has recently hit, you'll see page after page of ads for these individuals because they are so effective whenever insurance firms start to hedge on paying claims. The public adjuster is someone who is going to always help people get all that they are entitled to under the terms of the insurance coverage they have purchased. These folks get paid based on what they get for the insured (a percentage of the total loss - not over and above what the insurance companies pay), and so it is in your best interest to hire them, but also in theirs.

They don't get a huge sum, so don't look at them as mercenaries. Here's a pretty reasonable description of how it might work:

You get an insurance adjuster to evaluate your home. The insurance company extends an offer, and you think it is way off the mark. You ask them to review the entire matter and send a new adjuster out. They might refuse to budge on their offer.

Are your hands tied? No. You can still get in touch with a public adjuster who will look over the insurance policy, do an inspection and step up-to-bat to get you what you're due. Almost all of them are former insurance company adjusters who have since moved into the public sphere to work for the insured instead of the providers. They really know how to read the policies and already know where to look and see if you're getting short-changed by the insurance company. If the insurance company originally offered you something like $30,000 and the public adjuster got you another $10,000, the public adjuster gets a percentage of that $40,000.

They are not multimillionaires, yet insurance companies fear them because they are usually very informed, accurate and motivated. If you don't believe that insurance firms should fear them, just consider what the experts discovered during the study below.

20% to 35% OF ALL INSURANCE CLAIMS ARE WRONG
Only Six Out of Ten Claims are Accurate

The level of "wrongness" varied in the study because of different factors, but the primary issues that might impact a claim negatively were found to be:

- Inexperience on the part of the insurance adjuster.
- The sheer volume of material that most adjusters must manage in order to do a totally accurate claim.
- Lack of knowledge on the part of the adjuster for that type of disaster.

It's really okay to question the adjuster's findings and to pursue things as far as possible to get what you know you deserve. One sure way of doing that is to hire a public adjuster.

CHOOSING A PUBLIC ADJUSTER

How does this all work? The process begins when you contact your public insurance commissioner for the county or state (their contact information can be found online or in your phone book). **Find out the legal percentage that public adjusters can demand.** Usually it's going to be quite a range – anywhere between 5 to 50 percent of what they win for you.

Find out the cap in your area in order to do the most competitive shopping around. Start making a few calls and determine which have the best rates, and these are usually going to be somewhere in the "average" between the highest and lowest amounts.

Realistically, if the limit is around 10%, you may want to find someone in the 5-10% range. Just do the math and you may realize that even those at the higher end of the spectrum are not actually taking all that much. If the public adjuster does get you more, say $10,000 over the original offer and they ask for 10%, it would be 10% of the *total claim* - not of the difference. That means they got you more than the original amount, which is still pretty darn good. All things considered, this could be a *you get what you pay for* matter concerning public adjusters, so maybe don't go for the least expensive.

Is there any sort of insider's tip I can provide for you? Yes. If you have a friend or neighbor who used a public adjuster and was happy with their outcome, then ask for that adjuster's name and number.

Don't ask about the percentage first. Focus on their results. Word of mouth is a great way to get the contact information for an effective and successful public adjuster.

I can't tell you how many times I heard about people hiring someone because of a lower percentage and not their reputation, then being very unhappy with the outcome.

A second piece of advice I cannot emphasize enough is to ***be sure that you find out the legal percentage that a public adjuster can charge in your area.*** It can be very easy for someone to ask for too much and actually take it from you if they do get you to sign a contract.

Finally, understand that there are usually inexperienced adjusters of all kinds in high numbers doing the initial investigations after a storm.

This group includes inexperienced public adjusters.

THE ROOKIE ISSUE

To be certain that you have totally protected yourself before, during and after a disaster, we need to return for a moment to the issue of inexperienced adjusters. When I was itemizing the similarities and differences between contract FEMA inspectors and insurance adjusters earlier, I pointed out that in the days after a disaster, an area is going to see a dramatic increase in its overall "rookie head count". That is because both FEMA and the insurance firms want their top dogs back in the office doing things that maintain or create quality output.

Here's what I mean:

- Whenever there is a disaster, FEMA begins their work with a few days of training for all of the newly-recruited contract FEMA inspectors. They don't just toss the computer at them and say, "Good luck and Godspeed." Their top performers and most experienced contractors step up to do some of the training. That means they are not out in the field - one of the reasons for some delays and glitches when a disaster is first being handled. The good inspectors also have to spend time training others in the field doing "ride-a-longs". During big disasters, the most seasoned inspectors are out there working, but divide their time between ride-a-longs, reviews and inspections. The best of the best *are* in the field. They are simply reduced in their overall capacity to tackle the maximum numbers of actual inspections.
- When there is a disaster, the insurance companies need to get a fleet of adjusters out in the field, but they also don't want a lot of secondary claims or lawsuits because something was handled badly or wrong. In order to protect themselves from this, they keep a lot of their best adjusters in the office to review every single claim filed. If there is wrong or missing information on a claim, it is the seasoned adjuster's duty to turn it back over to the original adjuster until he or she gets it right. There are a lot of good seasoned adjusters out there in the field too.

That is not where the inexperienced adjuster story comes to an end. You already know that it is YOUR responsibility to really get a clear picture of the level of experience and expertise your adjuster has when he arrives. You know you need to ask them all of those questions about how long they've done the work, if they've handled this sort of disaster and so on. Simply being aware that you may have a rookie doing the job is an important first step. Then, if you think that you didn’t get a good inspection and aren't getting adequate responses from the insurance company, you already know that you can always get in touch with a public adjuster.

Here is where you have to exercise caution again. Remember, many rookies also come to this area too. Why? That has to do with the Insurance Commissioner. Usually after a major disaster, the commissioner or area office wants to be sure there is an adequate supply of adjusters to tackle the work. To do that, they put out the word that they are offering a "temporary adjuster's license" in the area where the disaster hit. This temporary licensing usually lasts for around 90 days and lifts the ban on people not certified for the work. This means they don't need training, qualifications and ongoing training. They are not even technically inexperienced, as they are usually fully trained. The people who get offered temporary licenses don't need to be experienced in any way.

For example, I worked in Louisiana after Hurricane Katrina where I saw for myself a flood of new contract FEMA inspectors being lured into the region. Soon, I watched a large number of these new inspectors just give up because of difficulties with the computers and the overall work. The insurance companies didn't help matters because they were frequently "poaching" the contract FEMA inspectors with offers of more lucrative work. Their earnings were based on getting the claim closed and their commission was a fixed amount such as $500 plus part of the insurance claim.

Inspectors left FEMA because there was a substantially higher profit margin, though it did demand a lot more work to do insurance claims. They had to assess the scope of damage, tackle the paperwork and use a range of computer programs to come up with viable offers. There's also a lot of back and forth with homeowners and insurance adjusters, but not for contract FEMA inspectors. The FEMA inspector is usually in and out and never goes back. An insurance adjuster might have to make many calls to a single homeowner before getting the claim closed in order to receive their commission.

A savvy homeowner will be aware of the fact that their contract FEMA inspector may not be the most experienced, and also that their insurance adjuster may also be someone newly recruited or poached without a history in their field. Also keep in mind that the smaller disasters - not like multi-state or multi-county ones like Hurricane Katrina or the Northridge Earthquake, or isolated incidents like tornadoes - may NOT require a lot of inexperienced hires. After these smaller disasters, you COULD get a very seasoned contract FEMA inspector as well as a top dog in the insurance adjuster field. If it is a "big one" though, DO remain aware of the inexperienced risks.

Why it is up to YOU to worry about and deal with the outcome of an inexperienced inspector or adjuster? That is a valid question, and here is the answer: If someone is hired or contracted by an insurance company and they botch the work, it is the insurance company that MUST take responsibility. They can only do this though if you are the one to call them out on it.

There could be a lousy assessment or even a radical case of "bad faith," and your insurance company could feasibly get away with it if YOU don't take the steps needed to hold them accountable. So, once again, it is that whole 50/50 issue. YOU have to own responsibility for yourself and get educated in order to provide yourself with adequate protection.

After all, the insurance companies have a lot of protection for themselves where these matters are concerned. They even purchase a form of insurance themselves (yes, insurance companies can also buy insurance) known as E & O insurance, formally known as Errors and Omissions insurance. This protects them from anything that an inexperienced adjuster might do wrong and any lawsuits or claims that could result. The 90-day lifting of restrictions on “newbies” mentioned earlier means that inexperienced adjusters hired by insurance companies are "their problem" and responsibility.

That is good news for everyone involved because insurance companies have purchased these large E & O policies. You may have to pursue a claim, but you won't have to worry about an independent adjuster not being liable for doing a lousy job. It is the insurance company's "bad" if that rookie screws up.

HURRICANE SANDY STORY
Why You Have to Do Your Homework!

A homeowner had his house insured for $250,000. Hurricane Sandy rolled ashore and his home was almost a total loss. The homeowner called FEMA and they instructed him to call his insurance company too (per FEMA rules). The homeowner called his insurance company and they told him they would send out an insurance adjuster as soon as possible who would start working on his claim. The homeowner was by now living in a hotel 25 miles away and needed to make arrangements to meet the adjuster. It had been about a week and no adjuster had called yet to make an appointment to come out and see his damages.

Meanwhile, the homeowner started to hear hundreds of stories about homeowners getting screwed by their insurance companies and not receiving anything at all or very little on their claims (the main reasons for these denials were that most people did not have flood insurance and received a “No Claim” letter and/or their damages didn’t meet their deductibles). After hearing so many horror stories, the homeowner panicked and began making mistakes he would not have made if he’d understood his *own* particular insurance coverage.

First, he called a public adjuster to negotiate his claim which, as you now know, is a great idea but can still come with some precautions. Once you get a public adjuster and sign his paperwork, YOU are out of the equation and he is now in full control of your claim. True, the adjuster does his best to get you the most money from your insurance company because the more he gets you, the more he makes. It should be a win-win situation, right?

However, the homeowner in this case never let the insurance company adjuster come into the mix and make him an offer. He found out later it would have been $240,000 of his $250,000 policy. The public adjuster in this case did his own calculation, came up with a figure, met with the insurance adjuster and informed him that he would not take less than than $160,000 from the insurance company. Unfortunately for the homeowner, the adjuster's job was to close as many claims as he could every day. That's his job, so the insurance adjuster says to him, "Sign here and here is your check for $160,000." The public adjuster was now happy as a clam, took the check back to the homeowner and handed it to him. They both seemed pleased with the amount until the public adjuster told the homeowner that HE needed to be paid his own percentage - 20% of the deal - which meant the homeowner had to give him $32,000 dollars for his efforts. This now left the homeowner with only $128,000 dollars. He later learned that according to the seasoned storm insurance adjuster's assessment, he actually incurred *$240,000* in real and personal property damages (or "structural and contents" in insurance terms).

The four things the homeowner did wrong in this example were:

1. He never let the insurance company make an offer. He should have done that first. If the offer was too low or not to his liking, that's the time to call a public adjuster.
2. He didn't quiz the public adjuster on his background or how long he had been doing insurance storm claims. He would have found out he was a rookie and inexperienced in this area.
3. He also could have called the Insurance Commissioner's office and found out how much a public adjuster was allowed to charge in this particular area on this disaster. It was mandated to be up to 10 percent, but the inexperienced adjuster took 20 percent. Most public adjusters were only charging 5 to 10 percent at this time.
4. He didn't do his homework and signed a contract for 20 percent!!

ELIMINATE SOME RISKS

How do you eliminate risks? In addition to doing your fair share of the work where knowledge of insurance company methods and responses is concerned, you also want to do all that you can to reduce your risks in general. For example, because there will probably be a lot of rookies in the field after a major disaster, you want to have a thorough understanding of your policy and what is covered. It also means you want to know what is inside your home and whether it is covered. Some of the following was explained to you in more detail earlier, but here is a summary of what my insurance industry buddies have all agreed on:

1. If you have homeowners insurance (and you'd be crazy not to), then check to see if it includes *ALE*: the Additional Living Expenses feature that will pay for a hotel or other form of housing and living expenses while you are waiting for your claim to be settled and your home to become livable again.
2. There is automatically no *ALE* available on any flood insurance policy. You will be asked to sign a document that indicates that all of the terms, limitations and other details of the flood insurance have been explained and that you accept them. I can assure you that 100% of

those policies are without any sort of *ALE*.

3. Find out if you can afford to purchase *ALE*. If you are buying flood insurance, you may be able to purchase some sort of *ALE* coverage. A friend in the insurance industry once told me that you can buy insurance for anything if you are willing to pay for it. If you are in an area prone to flooding or which has experienced severe hurricanes that led to disastrous flooding, consider if your budget might allow for some *ALE*. If not, be prepared to fund your own housing in the event of a flood. This will hold true even if it is a hurricane that led to flooding, or hope that FEMA will cover it if you're eligible.
   REMEMBER: Most insurance companies don't consider flooding as part of a hurricane. It is separate.
4. Purchase supplemental insurance if you have expensive things. People have lost valuable items where they will never receive compensation for because their homeowners insurance didn't cover them and they failed to purchase adequate supplemental insurance.
5. Create a household inventory in the environment of quiet and calm *before* a disaster strikes. Ask anyone who has experienced trauma of any kind. Your mind turns muddy; you're forgetful. Under these circumstances, would you remember everything you threw out after a flood? It's highly unlikely and furthermore, after a major disaster, it might take several weeks for the insurance adjuster to get to you. Be like the wealthy and receive a check for your loss faster because you prepared your household inventory checklist ahead of time and can just hand it over to the insurance adjuster when he or she arrives. Believe me...time is too important. They're not going to sit there while you complete it on the spot! Additionally, create:
   a. A video "tour" of your home. Use your phone or camera to walk through the entire house. Document the conditions in each of the rooms and try to really capture the overall quality of the interior. Do the same for the entire exterior of your home. Get shots of the roof and the windows to show their conditions too.
   b. A photographic inventory of special items as well as the entire home if you are going to buy policies for specific goods such as fur coats, gold coins, a couple of old pistols, a few paintings, etc. Accurately photograph each of them. Yes, it could take days to photograph a coin collection and create a binder that contains the proof of purchase for these coins, but if that house is wiped away by a flood and those coins go with it, your homeowners insurance is unlikely to give you the thousands or tens of thousands that washed down the river unless you are covered and can show detailed proof of the value of your loss.

Create that record (preferably a digital record) and store it in a safe place such as a "Cloud" or thumb drive, USB flash, CDR disc or on your smartphone. Or you could mail it to an out-of-state close relative. It's a good idea to keep records in a bank safety deposit box. Under no condition should you hand over your *only* copies of these items to the insurance company. There is NO reason for them to have the originals or the only copies. Make a few copies and even send one to your agent for his or her keeping if you want to, but keep the originals. And don't forget to review and update these each year to be certain that all of your expensive and valuable belongings are properly documented. It also is wise to include a binder or digital record of receipts for goods purchased whenever you can.

Let's say six months later you bought a stereo system that cost a lot of money. Copy the receipts and slip them into a sleeve in your home insurance binder. Take some pictures of it and add this to the inventory.

IMPORTANT NEW INFORMATION!

During final preparations to publish this book, ABC television network's *60 Minutes* broadcasted a report on June 7, 2015 about how thousands of Hurricane Sandy victims have still not received their insurance money for homes damaged during that storm which happened in October 2012.[5]

It appears that widespread fraud was committed - not with homeowners, but with the insurance companies falsifying the engineers' *original* reports, changing identified-structurally damaged properties into *no structural damage* noted. As of this writing, the jury is still out how this will be resolved between FEMA, the homeowners, insurance companies and the courts.

This is a prime example of where your due diligence comes in! Remember, when it comes to insurance companies paying out on claims, that buddy/buddy relationship you thought you had usually ends with dollar signs!

BE **FRECKS SMART** and do everything you can to protect yourself, your family and your property in the event you need to file a claim.

If this seems like a real hassle or if you don't have valuable items or digital equipment, make the trek down to your insurance company's local office and ask them for one of their household inventory pamphlets. All insurance companies offer these little "blank book" forms of documentation. Although they may be designed differently, these booklets will generally walk you through your entire home, room by room, and ask you to check off or document the number of specific items in each room. These pamphlets typically have pages for the kitchen, the living room, etc. On each page will be a list where you can write a number or use a check mark. It might include items such as lamps, TVs, computers, etc. This is a good way to gauge if you should start taking photographs of your more valuable goods as well. Taking this step helps ensure that the adjuster won't miss the most valuable goods and really streamlines the entire process.

Rather than arguing with them for days or weeks about the contents of your home, when you have your inventory done and all of the photographic and other evidence needed, it is simply a matter of handing them the copy of your inventory and waiting for them to do the rest. **Itemized household inventory checklists are included at the end of Section Three for your convenience.** If you don't want to do it yourself, some insurances companies offer to record your inventory and photograph the evidence for a small fee. Other companies also exist that can do this for you.

NOTE: Homeowners with itemized lists get their claims closed faster.

6. Visit your insurance company in person and go over "scenarios". This suggestion was made to me by a seasoned adjuster who told me it is the one true way to get an accurate picture of your insurance needs and coverage. It can even make the difference between someone easily overcoming a disaster or not.

Here's exactly what he said to do:

Go to your insurance company's office and ask your insurance agent if you can record the conversation if you want a transcript. Run through some scenarios with him or her. You will mention different events that could occur in your situation along with possible circumstances that could apply such as:

"A hurricane hits, my house is flooded and the entire downstairs is ruined. What happens with my current insurance coverage?" Or maybe, "I have homeowners insurance and we have a flood. Now the house has four feet of water inside. What am I covered for?"

You will get accurate answers straight from the horse's mouth. To the last question, an honest insurance agent would say, "Well, you wouldn't be covered with a homeowners policy because you are describing a flood."

You might then ask, "Oh, am I in a flood zone?"

A good agent would respond with, "Let's look at the map." The response should be telling you if you are in an A, B, C, D, etc. flood zone, and then whether or not your location deemed it necessary for coverage.

Even here your questions need to go on. For example, you say that you will buy flood insurance, but how much water would be covered? Double check the specifics that might apply, such as "where" did the water come from.

The best way to formulate a truly effective list of questions is to try to figure out ways that an insurance company might try to wiggle out of a full payment to you, the policyholder.

Make a long list of scenarios, run them all by the agent and make sure that you do this at least once each year or each time you change companies. It takes most people all of one full day to do the homework and legwork necessary to spare them from one of the biggest, longest and worst nightmares of their lives. Then, it might take an hour or two of your time each year to review your situation and possibly run some new scenarios over with your agent, but it is much better than finding yourself turning to a guy like me after a disaster, and saying,

"I paid this insurance for like 40 years and I never knew I wasn't covered and they never told me!"

When someone says that to me, I tell them that I'm sorry to hear it, but I'm also thinking, "Well, shame on you! Why didn't you know what was covered and what wasn't?"

7. If a disaster does strike, get out your camera once again. No matter what sort of disaster you have just endured, you have to pull yourself together as quickly as you can and start to document the scope of your damage. Try to mentally recall all of the shots you originally took for your household inventory or video tour, and then retrace those steps again on those same items. Try to get close-up images of all problems, damages and losses. Include images of all the goods in your home too in order to have indisputable proof that the damages did occur.

Why? Isn't it going to be easy to show the damages? The answer is no. This is because it could take weeks for your adjuster to get to you.

Most disaster victims won't want to wallow around in the mess and filth left by a disaster. Most people attempt to pick up the pieces within hours or days of the incident. That means that you could mistakenly erase the damages *just by cleaning up!*

Even as you are carrying stuff out of the house and piling it at the curb, take photos. As you sort through debris, take photos. As you begin to make any repairs, document the hell out of the "before and after" of your efforts. Get photos, videos, keep receipts and retain all of the evidence you will need to show that your damages were real and true and that you simply tried to make your home livable as soon as possible, even as you waited for the adjusters to come. A disaster scene is not the same as a crime or accident where the "scene" has to remain untouched. You can begin to make repairs right away, but don't even lift a hammer or pick up garbage without first doing extreme documentation of everything and of every step you take.

You can never take too many photos. Yes, it sounds excessive, but if you have an insurance firm try to pull a bit of "bad faith" on you, it is best to have reams of evidence to demonstrate that they are willfully declining your claim when the damage and loss did most certainly occur. Try also to include a newspaper with the day's date and headlines in the shots. This will show that your photos or footage are not a few years old or some other nonsense that could be argued to deny your claim.

8. Get yourself a copy of the Flood Insurance Claims Handbook.[6] You can often get this at an insurance office or go online and download it to your computer. It is an ideal resource for anyone who needs help with what to do before, during and after a flood of any kind. Having a handbook like this is going to help the homeowner, but will also help the insurance company to handle any claims in a much better way. My friend in the insurance industry thinks it's odd that people don't just pick up this book. It is an amazing resource and something that everyone should know about. In fact, I agree with him so much that I carry copies of this handbook with me when doing contract FEMA inspections to give out to people when I see they could benefit from it. Written in layman's terms, this resource really does have all the answers to the most common questions. It also contains information in the back similar to the lists provided for you in Section Three of this book.
9. Another handy tool to pick up is something known as the ICC or Increased Cost of Compliance Coverage book.[7] It's not really a book, but more of a brochure from FEMA and the National Flood Insurance Program. It was written to help with relocating, raising or demolishing a dwelling in a flood zone of a participating community per code standards.
10. Understand which additional coverages you might need and what forms are available. I say this mostly because I know what people in Florida go through whenever there is a disaster. Many Floridians don't realize the long list of insurance "types" they actually should have. These include homeowners, flood, hurricane, wind, pool and more. There are also people living in California and other states who don't realize they might need to purchase earthquake insurance and end up not covered in the event of a quake. It is part of your responsibility to know all that you can about disasters that could occur in your area and if you can get coverage for them. Earthquake insurance in California could even be mandatory per your mortgage company, but if you are not carrying a mortgage, you might let it lapse, then face some pretty serious and very sad consequences. Even when you can get coverage for some of the most common disasters in your area, there may also be some changes in the coverage that make it less desirable. For example, there are some earthquake policies that only cover 50% of the structural damages and 50% of the contents of the home. That might not be enough to allow someone to recover, yet you may be unable to avoid the problem.

A BIG EXAMPLE

If you want a big example of why you need to find ways to reduce or eliminate risks to yourself before, during and after a disaster, I will provide you with a very good illustration. Here's how it goes:

A lot of insurance companies do not perform a full formal inspection of a home or property before they issue a policy. Sometimes they just drive by or send someone to snap a photograph or two. Then an agent reviews this and begins to write the policy. That means that it is ultimately up to YOU, the owner of the property, to be 100% sure that the policy is okay. That means making certain that the insurance company has everything from the style of the roof to the composition of the structure entirely accurate. Yes, it does seem like it should be THEIR job to get it right, but when the chips are down, they will definitely throw you under the bus and let you take the blame or suffer the consequences for NOT making certain that all the information was correct.

Today, things are even worse in the modern era of online insurance quotes. You can keep adjusting details until you see the figure you are comfortable with, but that NEVER means that you are covered in the right way. It doesn't even guarantee that your claims filed on that policy will hold up. After all, if you check off the "hip roof" box when you actually have a flat roof, it means that you gave false information and therefore the company doesn't have to pay one penny on a claim of damages to the home in a storm or other disaster. In fact, "fraud" of that kind could negate your policy entirely.

Instead of just breezing through this part of obtaining homeowner's insurance and any additional coverage, take the time to scrutinize each of the details to be certain all is correct. There are now even companies that send out agents to help you do the best assessment of your property long before a disaster strikes. This can help you take in all of the different factors involved and calculate just how much it would realistically cost you to rebuild, repair or replace your home and its contents. This could also be an ideal resource for identifying the various factors that could negate a claim. For example, this type of service would help you understand the style of roof, building materials, etc. A good example of this was the "My Safe Florida Home" program offered through FEMA and the State of Florida. I was one of those inspectors paid to provide free inspections of homes throughout the entire state of Florida. This program came about because of the catastrophic 2004 hurricane season when four major hurricanes hit. After that, the state as well as FEMA wanted to help people remain safe and also see homes constructed to much better standards for that area.

"My Safe Florida Home" display inside a Lowe's store

The insurance companies had taken substantial "hits" at that time, and this "forced" them to raise everyone's rates; not by a few hundred bucks, but by thousands in some cases. It was determined that it would be in everyone's best interest to find ways of reducing risks in general.

We set up informational booths in places like Home Depot where people could learn about the program and book an inspection. As an inspector, I would go out to the property and do an assessment that would ensure it was as "hurricane resistant" as possible. This meant I was looking at the design of the roof. Was it a gable end? If it was, this was a red flag because hurricanes and gable end roofs are not the best companions. I also looked at the nail patterns, the plywood, the inside of the attic and its nail pattern. Were the rafters clipped down, was bracing in place, was the garage door hurricane resistant? Did the house have the right front door bolt assemblies? What sort of hurricane shutters were on the house, and so on. The list of items was very extensive, but it was something a homeowner could do to proactively prepare for a disaster and be sure they were paying for the right kind of insurance.

Essentially, it was all the things that could save a house - any kind of house. I was to look at everything and explain it to the homeowners. Not only did this assessment inform them of any weaknesses that were in the home, but it also came with a rating. When a homeowner got a high rating, it meant they received a better rate on their insurance. This FREE program effectively helped people prepare as well as discover if their insurance was both accurate and priced at the best rate possible.

Of course, the flip side also sometimes occurred and a lot of the homeowners called me in shock that their insurance rates had been raised. But as they complained and told me the insurance company's explanations for the increases, I had all that I needed to justify the rating. "Oh, you had a gable roof that wasn't fitted with hurricane clips or diagonal bracings in the attic. That's why the rate went up. That roof is likely to blow off in a storm!"

Usually this would not calm the customer down, but then I would give them the reality. "Okay," I would say calmly. "You're all up in arms because your rates went up, but what if there had already been a storm? If your house was damaged or ruined, the insurance company could have easily denied your claim and left you high and dry because of 'inaccurate' information." This usually straightened it out because I was giving them the facts.

Using a service like this and knowing all of the factors that affect coverage beforehand might inspire homeowners to make some of the upgrades necessary to stabilize and protect the house and possibly qualify for a better rating.

Use these freebies if and when you can, and definitely hire someone that offers this service if you are in an area prone to disasters such as hurricanes. It is a very good, inexpensive and sometimes no-cost way to protect your house and find out if you are properly insured.

Believe me when I tell you that the insurance companies will never take this sort of step for you. It is always going to be up to you, although do keep in mind that things are changing a bit. Some insurance companies are footing the bill for these inspections, but even then, there are "expiration dates" on them. I still get calls from people whose homes I inspected years ago because they see that the five-year time limit is drawing near and they want a new inspection. Also be aware that these inspections are not a one-shot deal. You need to review them every few years and get it redone whenever your current inspection is considered to have expired. And yes again, it will be entirely up to you to keep track of the dates, deadlines and other details. As we already know, this is part of YOUR 50% obligation of responsibility.

WHAT'S THE PAYOFF?

I can already hear you asking, "I do all of this work and so what is the payoff?" I have already explained that you might get the best results possible if you have an inspection. Even if you don't have that detailed review, doing all of this preliminary work often means that you can get funding from the insurance company extremely fast. For example, if you hand them a binder with all of the inventory information and you have that preliminary inspection done which guarantees your coverage is adequate and accurate, plus you started to document anything you did before an adjuster arrives, it is entirely possible that you'll get some or all of the money you are due almost immediately. Realistically, that is the entire point of having insurance in the first place: to give you the money that you need to make repairs or to entirely rebuild if something disastrous happens to your home. Your efforts could ensure that you have a good place to live, that you get compensated for lost valuables and antiques, that you're not overpaying and that you get the most precise dollar amount for the claim you submit.

Obviously, all of the above would be an ideal outcome, but if you don't get yourself educated about insurances, don't make any preliminary plans, don't organize yourself ahead of time and don't ensure that your home and insurances are in alignment, you can face a lot of challenges.

Fortunately, we have gone over all of the things you need to do even when faced with serious problems from the insurance company in order to get the money you deserve and to protect yourself. You now know how to protect yourself from the insurance companies and from yourself.

INSIDER TIDBITS THEY WON'T TELL YOU...

I also have a few little tidbits that I need to give you. They are pretty important, even if these are odds and ends insurance companies may not ever tell you.

These include the following after a disaster:

- KEEP YOUR RECEIPTS. Receipts! Receipts! You can never have enough receipts. Keep every single one. Ask yourself, "Did the storm make me buy this?" No matter how insignificant a purchase might seem to be: food, water, clothing, gasoline, hotel, any bill you pay - even bridge tolls you pay to get replacement materials for rebuilding - anything! You will need to have a paper trail of every expenditure. If you do not have receipts for FEMA and for your insurance company, they will most likely not reimburse you. Even credit card receipts will work. **NOTE:** Black out your credit card number and all expenses NOT included in the disaster.
- KEEP ALL RECEIPTS FOR YOUR TAXES. In a federally declared disaster zone, the IRS may allow you to deduct up to 100% of expenses to help you recover after a disaster on your taxes, but you MUST have receipts. Again, credit card receipts will work.
- NAMED STORMS USE A HIGHER DEDUCTIBLE. "What?!" I hear you say, but my insurance buddies confirmed it. When a storm (such as a tropical storm or a hurricane) gets an official name from the weather agencies, it bumps the deductibles up under the terms of many insurance policies. This is one of those "scenarios" you'll want to pose to your insurance agent. Your question can sound like this: "So, if an unnamed tropical storm rolls through and does damage, will my deductible still be the same if 'Hurricane Bob or Zelda or Herman' hits in the same year?" This is as plain-speak as it can get and will force the agent to provide a direct answer about any such terms in your coverage.
- THINK BEFORE YOU CALL - AND I MEAN BEFORE YOU CALL *ANYONE!* This is because a "No Claim" from the insurance

company is a Catch 22 situation. If you call FEMA first, they make you call the insurance company. However, calling the insurance company may result in a No Claim, even if the damage is catastrophic because you might not have had the coverage for the damage (i.e., no flood insurance). This now puts you at risk for higher rates or even being dumped altogether. Additionally, you may be forced to buy a specific type of insurance that you may be unable to afford. As an example, some of the people who lost homes or suffered enormous damages due to Hurricane Sandy are now required to have annual flood insurance policies. If that large annual sum for flood insurance is not in their budgets, they only have the other option of rebuilding by raising the home 12 feet (using concrete pillars). This is obviously not a good set of choices, but that is where the insurance companies left people who made claims. Because of possibilities such as this, you want to determine if this is a can of worms you want to open when you go without insurance and then make a phone call.

- You will only get, at the very most, around $30,000 from FEMA if you qualify and meet their criteria for eligibility. They are not similar to insurance, they do not duplicate anything that an insurance company will pay and they obligate you to call the insurance company in order for them to send a storm adjuster out. There is no double dipping with FEMA and insurance.
- If you receive FEMA Disaster Assistance on a flood disaster, FEMA makes it mandatory to carry flood insurance for that dwelling for as long as you reside in that dwelling.
- Even after a disaster hits, a large number of people still do NOT prepare for a future disaster. With free inspections or affordable insurance reviews available, with all kinds of steps that can be taken to protect themselves, and even in the face of multiple disasters and storms, it is not uncommon for homeowners to still remain totally vulnerable. As an example, I will point to Florida again. Even with four hurricanes in a year, many billions in losses and ongoing hikes in insurance rates, a recent study discovered that around 70% of people there have no plan in place where hurricanes are concerned. They might not even have an escape plan, any emergency supplies set aside or any sort of legwork done to protect them from insurance problems should something go down. Lots of people don't even know whether or not they are in a flood zone and what impact this might have on them should disaster strike.

RECEIPTS! RECEIPTS! RECEIPTS!

A local news station put me in touch with a Katrina victim nine years after the disaster. Both FEMA and the IRS had attached his income tax check and wages to repay money he received after relocating to my area. After talking to the victim, I discovered HE HADN'T SAVED ANY RECEIPTS to prove his losses. If you don't save receipts, as far as FEMA or the IRS is concerned, it never happened or you didn't buy it!

You have to create a paper trail. Never give your original receipts to FEMA or the IRS. They'll lose them! I always tell victims to make 4 or 5 copies before you send them in because most assuredly, FEMA will lose them 3 or 4 times. Don't bother sending in your receipts certified mail either. The same scenario will happen.

Using your credit card provides you with a receipt, but after most major disasters, retail stores may not have power. No power, no receipt. Ask the store to handwrite one out for you. If your purchase was storm-related, most likely it could be up to 100% deductible on your year-end tax return.

You may even be able to deduct evacuation expenses on your taxes. Keep all of your receipts because you never know what will be covered from one disaster to another. If you get audited, you'll want to have as many receipts as possible to cover any monies FEMA gave you.

People always ask me, "How do I know what receipts to keep?"

Basically, all of them, including such things as gas to run a generator, but a trip to Hawaii to relieve stress after a disaster strikes is not one of them!

And as this gentleman found out, keep them for years and years after the disaster happened. You have no idea when you'll need them.

WRAPPING IT UP

I have given you an insider's perspective on all things insurance. You should be able to take steps to protect yourself from any business thrown your way by the insurance companies. You are now also able to sidestep any problems that you might have unknowingly caused yourself. Though we've already gone over everything in great detail, let's just summarize what you need to know:

- An ounce of prevention is worth its weight in gold. Take your share of the responsibility and make sure your home is prepared.
- It's up to you to protect yourself. Don't go on faith that your insurance company is your pal or keeping you in good and safe arms. They may not. You must do all of the preliminary legwork and research needed to guarantee that you receive the best possible outcome from any damages your home or property suffers. It is a 50/50 venture, and the

sooner you accept that, the better off you will be.

- Pose "scenarios" to your insurance agent in order to find out just what exactly your homeowners insurance covers and how you can fill in the gaps with other types of coverage.
- Perform a home inventory that includes video and digital photos. Document every possible facet of your home, contents and other possessions. Fill out the inventory sheets located in the back of this book.
- Buy supplemental coverage for costly household goods that a normal policy will not cover.
- Make copies of your household inventory, update it as needed and **never** give your originals to the insurance company.
- Document everything you do in the hours and days after a disaster. This eliminates any chance of you being declined compensation for the work done to make necessary initial repairs.
- Get your hands on the different handbooks and pamphlets suggested in this chapter. They are excellent tools before, during and after a disaster to ensure that you've covered all of your bases.
- Pay for someone to do an insurance assessment or look for one of the low-cost home inspection companies that are meant to help you get your home into tip-top condition before anything happens.
- Know if you should have fire, flood, earthquake, wind and any other of these "special" policies.
- Know that storms given names mean higher deductibles.
- Have plans in place, including a survival kit with an absolute minimum of three days of supplies (see Section Three of this book).
- There are many similarities between a seasoned insurance adjuster and a contract FEMA inspector. The main thing to remember is that both of them always report the facts and attempt to remain as neutral as possible. Even when both are experienced and know their stuff, it can still be challenging for them to get everything just right unless the owner is there and knows enough to help facilitate the process.
- It is common for a lot of rookies to be in the field when a major disaster hits. Be aware of this and be prepared to do your own due diligence. Question their experience when they arrive.
- There is a HUGE difference between Insurance and FEMA. Insurance is there to help you rebuild, replace and repair. Insurance is something you have paid for personally for years, but it has a much broader scope than FEMA, which is an essential needs program funded by tax dollars. They will try to help you live in your home after a disaster, but their scope is far more limited.
- The terms of an insurance policy are in YOUR hands and it is entirely up to you to know IF:
  - You are over insuring.
  - You have adequate coverage for your needs.

- You have the right types of insurances.
- You are in a flood zone, and if so, which flood zone.
- You are in any disaster zones – tornado, earthquake, hurricane, fire, etc.
- You are in need of supplemental insurance for valuable goods.
- Your property is described precisely accurate in the insurance documents or if you are way off the mark and therefore, open to a complete negation of coverage.
- You are aware of the whole “deductible” and "cost" issue. Are you paying for a lower premium and putting yourself at risk with a deductible that is too high for you to afford? Have you considered what it will actually cost you if a disaster occurs?
- You are covered for *ALE*.
- Insurance adjusters are subcontracted and are not working "for" or "in favor of” the insurance companies. There are penalties that can arise when an insurance company behaves badly, wrong or unfairly. An adjuster is never willingly or knowingly part of this pattern of behavior.
- Are you clear on the outcome of making a call to either FEMA or an insurance company? There are many problems this can cause including higher premiums, etc. Are you clear on what might transpire if you pursue any sort of FEMA assistance or file a claim with your insurance company?

There are several steps to take when you are unhappy with the outcome of a visit by an adjuster:

- DICKER: You can debate the figures they offer and keep asking for a new review when you find discrepancies in their offer.
- GO FOR AN SBA LOAN WHILE DICKERING: This is step two of the first step for those prepared to take a 1-5% interest SBA loan on a federally declared disaster which can allow you to rebuild while you argue with an insurance firm.
- DISPUTE YOUR SCOPE OF LOSS: This is a mild approach to getting what you deserve. The adjuster may have overlooked or neglected something and most of these disputes are quickly resolved.
- THE APPRAISAL: Asking for an appraisal brings neutral parties into the mix and guarantees that the insurance company is likely to back down and try to make you happy without going all the way on the appraisal.
- FILE A FORMAL COMPLAINT TO THE INSURANCE COMMISSIONER: This is something you must take seriously because everyone, even you, will be investigated. However, this is such a serious move that most insurance companies will sit up and listen to when you say you plan to file such a complaint.

- BAD FAITH: This is the mother of all complaints because it puts the company at risk for two to ten times the amount due as a penalty. They really, and I emphasize again REALLY, don't want this to happen.
- THE PUBLIC ADJUSTER: This too is the mother of all methods because it brings in an outside party who has a vested interest in getting the most out of the insurance company. These are people who know how to read policies and scrutinize the offers. They ask for a percentage of what the total amount of the claim is - not an extra amount they get for you above what was offered by the insurance company. Usually, it's a win-win situation.

Frecks' Fast Tips About Insurance Policies

1. Understand how to read the Declarations Page of your policy.
2. Shop around for insurance every year at renewal time to make sure you're getting a good rate based on your coverage.
3. Ask your insurance agent questions if you don't understand any section of your insurance policy.

Don't take anything for granted. Insurance agents who sell homeowners (and vehicle) policies work on a commission basis and sometimes pad your policy with extras and no explanation why in order to increase your premium. Some agents are honest, but let the buyer beware!

ONE MAN'S BATTLE
It Pays to Know

A bit earlier I mentioned the fires in California, a good example of how it's a 50/50 issue where insurances are concerned. If you don't know just what is covered, you can't say that the insurance companies are wrong or evil. Read your policies. Once you know what you're supposed to be getting, it can still often be up to you to pursue what is fair for you to the fullest extent.

This was exactly the case in California where one man knew that he was due a specific amount, but had to go to great lengths just to get what was rightfully his. The way it worked out was this:

His home had been burned to the ground in the fires. His insurance company kept sending offers that were far less than what they should have been. Not small beans here, folks. We're talking a huge difference of over $200k. They actually sent him a denial letter for certain claims as well.

Initially, he lived in a tent in his front yard, even though he practiced as a medical professional. Rather than succumbing to the pressures and delays, he used an alternative option open to almost everyone. He went ahead and applied for FEMA because they have disaster SBA loans available.

Where else can you get such a great deal with a 1-5 percent interest rate? He knew that he would eventually settle with the insurance company and would then use that sum to pay the SBA loan back in full.

BE FRECKS SMART!

Eighty percent of all disaster work is flood-related.

The average flood insurance policy costs about $500 a year. The average flood insurance claim is about $32,000 dollars.

Which would you rather pay?

SBA LOAN OPTIONS

This is something we have not touched upon yet. Through FEMA, the SBA (Small Business Administration) can give disaster loans. Remember, these are *loans*, not grants. Be aware that FEMA gives people up to $30k in grants, but that is rarely enough to rebuild a home.

The SBA disaster loans, on the other hand, can be borrowed for up to $200k if needed. Homeowners and renters can also borrow up to $40k to replace personal property, including vehicles.

You DO have to fill out a FEMA application to gain access to SBA loan options. You will still need to have a FEMA inspection done. Usually, the SBA informs you within a day or two whether you qualify for the loan.

If you qualify, an SBA agent will come to your home and perform an inspection of the damages, then come up with a figure to help rebuild your home.

This guy involved with the California fires used a proactive approach and kept up the battle with his insurance company as he used the funds of the SBA loan to rebuild. It took more than two years for the entire process to be completed, but because he was a medical professional, he needed to maintain a normal home life to work in his practice each day rather than live in a tent.

The point here is that you can pursue alternative paths for rebuilding your life. The insurance companies don't own you or your destiny. Though there is the risk of being dropped or having rates increased when a claim is made, you

DID buy insurance.

You are due a fair return on that investment, and if it means using a complex method like this man did, so be it!

WHAT'S HAPPENING AT INSURANCE COMPANIES TODAY

The information provided below was relayed to me through one of my insurance company colleagues. Bear in mind that the Flood Protection Program portion of insurance is actually run by FEMA, but is administered through private insurance companies. And as you'll learn later at the end of Section Two, a similar scenario is now happening with seasoned FEMA inspectors.

Lately, the insurance companies have been implementing changes to one of its most important commodities, the seasoned insurance adjuster.

In the recent past few catastrophes, the pay scales offered to perform inspections on claims were cut, less claims were given out to perform the inspections and excessive amounts of paperwork was added to the mix. Many insurance storm adjusters wonder if they matter to their insurance companies anymore. Additionally, the insurance companies and insurance adjuster firms are hiring out the processing of claims to less qualified people who sit in their desk cubicles and have no real insurance background or no solid construction experience to speak of. They approve "cookie cutter" claims and/or deny others because they don't look the same as other claims to them and they cannot differentiate between an accurate claims written by actual claims adjusters because they don't possess the experience.

The insurance companies and insurance storm adjuster firms make an enormous amount of money by not paying qualified adjusters. At this time, many insurance adjusters I know will not go out on catastrophes anymore. They have two households to pay for when they are at a disaster site and are not receiving enough claims to cover the costs of travel, hotel, food, gas, insurance and all of the other costs that are almost always at a premium during a disaster. Many companies are trying to pay an hourly wage, but that doesn't come close to what actual costs are for an insurance adjuster.

The actuaries in the corporate structure work by numbers alone and not in real costs. I am afraid that now and in the future, people will not be paid what is actually owed to them when they file a claim. The bottom line is, soon there will be no adjusters to take care of the people. As it is now, the insurance companies and insurance adjuster firms have cut pay so badly and limited the amount of claims that an adjuster receives that no one but the unemployed person living at home with their parents that just quit their job at a fast food restaurant will be able to work as an adjuster.

The insurance companies would rather pay less and have the insured file a supplement for what they actually have lost. This puts a burden on the insured and most will not file the supplement, and then the insurance company doesn't have to pay the actual loss.

How comfortable can this make a disaster victim feel when the insurance adjuster hasn't a clue what type of wall finishes are in the home or what type of carpet was damaged?

Adjusters, another product of corporation tactics, are people too.

Phew! Now you have it all. You can no longer say that you didn't know about any of these matters and can take a lot of informed, strong empowering steps to shore up your home and protect yourself in every way possible from the questionable maneuvers that insurance companies might attempt, as well as the trouble that you might cause for yourself!

Now, let's take a REALLY close look at FEMA's essential needs program and how your cooperation is crucial to your financial benefits aid.

SECTION TWO

HOW TO HELP FEMA HELP YOU

HOW TO GET A GOOD FEMA INSPECTION

HELP ME TO HELP YOU

Did you know that you and your FEMA inspector are a "team"? You can work with him or her to quickly and effectively obtain the help you need.

People sometimes become stressed by their situation and release a torrent of frustration at me, but I say this, "C'mon! Just help me to help you!" You have to see yourself as working *with* the inspector.

Is it that simple? Yes, but a lot of people are impacted adversely by the disaster, unaware that the CFI is operating under a serious time limit and generally don't understand what an inspector is supposed to see/learn/do. They become a hurdle to the process.

With that thought, next is a lesson in *How to Help Me to Help You.*

PREPARE

What you do before a disaster occurs is important in how easy your disaster recovery goes. You may have heard about disaster preparedness kits.[8] They are crucial and shouldn't just include food, water and first aid, but important documents too!

Create a FEMA file before a disaster occurs. This is almost identical to the insurance files mentioned before. Here is a complete list of the documents you might need:

A. Photo ID: an official government issued ID (such as a driver's license, military ID, passport, etc.).
B. Personal identifying information for everyone who lives in the home: Names, ages, social security numbers and birth dates.
C. Proof of home ownership (including deed, title, tax bill, mortgage payment book, etc.).
D. Square footage of your home (very helpful to the CFI).
E. Your insurance policy's Declaration Page (whether for a homeowners or renter's policy).
F. Proof of occupancy (utility bill, merchant bills, paycheck stubs, driver's license with the correct address or voter registration). **NOTE:** FEMA applications are for a primary residence only. You will not be able to submit an application for anything other than your primary place of residence. You must currently live in that

home (for at six months and one day out of the calendar year) for it to qualify as a primary residence. Let's say that you own a property in Puerto Rico and spend six months and two weeks there every year. That would be considered your primary residence. If your other home is in West Virginia and you spend the rest of the year there, it would not qualify as a primary residence because you were there less than six months and one day in that year. If the place you list as your primary residence is not where you get your mail, you must indicate this on the form to ensure that you get all of the information from FEMA - including the check - if you are not using direct deposit (provided you qualify for assistance). If your primary residence has been totally destroyed by the disaster, you'll need to provide a different address where you can get mail.

G. Phone numbers: primary phone, cell phone, backup phone, work, etc. FEMA asks for four different numbers, and I beg you to make sure they are all active numbers. There is nothing so frustrating as trying to call an applicant and getting a series of disconnected or non-working numbers.

H. Email address: Make sure this is your primary valid email address. Double check the spelling. Remember that you can use a lot of resources to access email. You can get it on your smartphone, through a public computer at a library and even at some emergency services, such as at the Fire Department who generally allows people to use their computers to check email.

I. Automobile information - Registration and Insurance: If you sustain damages to vehicles as a result of the disaster, FEMA will want to know about it. They do not accept the little "Proof of Insurance" cards you keep in your glove box or wallet. Instead, they want the policy Declarations Page.
NOTE: Don't worry if the car has been towed away or is located somewhere else.

J. Know your total household income.

K. Your bank account and routing numbers: FEMA can directly deposit your assistance check into your account within a day or two after your inspection if you qualify. I know some people feel compromised passing this information out freely and worry about giving "The Feds" access to their account, but it can get you the assistance you qualify for almost immediately. Alternately, FEMA can send you a regular check in the mail (which can take a long time after a disaster).

L. Just like you would do for insurance purposes, create a video and photographic inventory of everything of value on your property. Assemble an itemized inventory of all electronics, TV, stereo, refrigerator, washer, dryer along with any identifying numbers such as serial numbers. Also, if you have an outbuilding where you have put utility equipment or appliances, document that room and the condition of it as well.

M. Provide a description of your losses that occurred due to the disaster. This description should highlight all of your losses without going into too much detail. The inspector who comes out to the property will document the extent of damages and how it occurred with photographic evidence and a detailed proof report.

Assure yourself that you will have access to your documentation after a disaster. This is something many people probably won't do, but I can guarantee you it will make a tremendous difference in your life if you do it now. Prepare this emergency file and then scan it into your computer (or save it in your Cloud service if you have one) or in your cell phone. You can also email yourself each of the documents and just leave them in your Inbox.

Another clever thing to do is install a FAX app on a smartphone or tablet. You might receive paperwork after the disaster occurs and may be asked to fax some of it back to FEMA. As an example, your insurance company could send you a denial letter or "No Claim" notice. FEMA will want to see it. If you installed the app on your smartphone, you could use the camera to take a clear image of the letter, then attach it using the app. Also, you can use a phone to snap a photo of the document and, if you've linked your email account to your phone, you'll be able to attach it to an email and send it that way.

Accept that you will still have some challenges. Even if you have taken all of my advice and prepared yourself before disaster strikes, you probably will face technical challenges in the days or weeks after a disaster, particularly because Wi-Fi and cell services may not be up and running. Know that there are emergency centers set up by organizations such as FEMA and the Red Cross, and some of them have these options available.

If you have a FEMA file created, it is easier to prepare for FEMA's arrival on the scene. When a disaster occurs, locate your FEMA file/Disaster Kit before you sit down to call FEMA.

Here are other things you need to do to prepare for a FEMA inspection:

- Change your voice mail message! If at all possible, it should say something as simple as, "You've reached [insert name]. Please leave a message." Remove long or musical messages until you've booked your FEMA appointment.
- Take "After" photos. When a disaster has occurred, take photos and videos of the conditions *after* the disaster, during cleanup and as you recover. This is especially important if you know that your CFI is going to be unable to get to you right away. Use photos to try and document a water line if your home is flooded by

photographing somewhere that has a point of reference - such as a wall with a door or even a table leg in order to give an accurate idea of how high the water went. Though an experienced inspector has a lot of skill in determining water lines, it's much better to have it officially documented.

- Determine whether or not you will need to relocate. If you must relocate, make sure you have all of the pertinent paperwork and receipts to present to your FEMA inspector. You may qualify for housing assistance - a big part of assistance FEMA provides.
- Itemize your losses. Make a list. List all of the things that you know happened to the home, the items that were destroyed or are missing and things that were seriously damaged. The inspector is also going to ask you about essential personal property damages. This is something people tend to undervalue. For example, the home that has three to four inches of water on the first floor may have a lot of essential personal property destroyed. This could be a TV, refrigerator, washer/dryer or a dining table ruined in the disaster. It could be clothing. If you qualify for assistance, you may receive some funds to replace those essential items.
- Save all receipts to show what you have paid for in any disaster-related cleanup and/or repairs fixed such as drywall, insulation, nails, paint and personal property. Other possible items include miscellaneous purchases, visits to the doctor, dentist or funeral expenses. All of these things can possibly be considered by the IRS as tax deductible.

  NOTE: Consult a CPA with federally declared disaster tax knowledge or visit a Disaster Recovery Center (DRC) for information on tax relief.
- While FEMA or your insurance company may not be able to reimburse you for all of these things, they help to demonstrate that you qualify for assistance. You also need this itemization for your taxes.

OWNERS VS RENTERS

Before you do any clean up at all, know that there are different inspection types depending on whether you are a renter or an owner. FEMA looks at an owner's property based on the damage immediately following the storm, not based on the way it appears visually on the day of the inspection. Make sure to document everything with photographs and receipts.

Personal property damage for owners and renters are recorded as they existed *immediately* following the event.

However, **Housing assistance** is different for owners. For owners, it is based on real property damage as it existed immediately following the event. For renters, it is based on damages that have not been repaired *at the time of* *the inspection.*

Write down any questions you might have. You can get stage fright when the inspector arrives and miss important questions that you wanted to ask. In the wake of a disaster, is anyone thinking clearly?

Let neighbors know that you have applied and encourage them to do so. If you and your neighbors privately own the access road to your properties, FEMA may provide assistance to make necessary repairs if everyone has applied and is eligible for assistance.

DISASTER RECOVER CENTERS (DRC)

I strongly advocate that anyone involved in a disaster makes a point of going to FEMA's Disaster Recovery Center (DRC), a wealthy resource for emergency information. You will find a nearly endless assortment of pamphlets dealing with all of the subjects that come up when a disaster hits. Additionally, the Red Cross usually resides somewhere in the parking lot area and sometimes provides food and/or supplies.

You can find SBA people offering loans, and they can complete the loan paperwork with you. You can also apply for FEMA assistance there. The DRC is a major resource that too few disaster victims utilize.

Here are some other examples of what the DRC offers:

- Guidance regarding disaster recovery.
- Clarification of any correspondence you received.
- Housing assistance and rental resource information.
- Answers to questions, resolution of problems or referrals to other agencies that may offer assistance to you.
- The status of applications being processed by FEMA.

Other helpful services include:

1. SBA Program Information[9]
2. Crisis Counseling Program[10]
3. Disaster Legal Services (DLS)[11]
4. Disaster Unemployment Benefits[12]
5. Funeral Assistance – Individuals and Household Programs[13]

APPLY

Contact FEMA as soon as you have all of your information in hand. You can contact them by phone or the web.

Make the call! Just like the lottery's motto, "You can't win if you don't play!" To call from anywhere in the United States (or in any United States territory declared a federal disaster zone), phone them at: 800-621-3362. YOU must get the ball rolling.

If you are fortunate enough to have an internet connection, it's easy to apply online for assistance through their website at http://www.FEMA.gov. I encourage anyone with computer access to use this route. If you have gathered up all of the documents listed above, just hop online and begin the entire process there.

Provide all of the necessary information. Most importantly, give FEMA a way to reach you! Double check the number that you give over the phone or type into the computer. Ask the FEMA phone operator to repeat the phone number(s) at least once before hanging up. If you're one who doesn't answer the phone when you don't recognize a number, give FEMA the number of a family member who can instantly get in touch with you.

Take down the Control Number. When you apply, whether over the phone or online, you will receive a nine-digit control number. This is assigned exclusively to your case and you must have it handy at all times. Be sure you ask for it when applying by phone and write it down. If applying online, your control number will be assigned to you during the application process. Keep track of this number because it's also used by other agencies. In order to get food stamps, you must have this number to prove you've applied for FEMA assistance. You will also need it at the DRC.

Read the Privacy and Declaration Statements if applying online. I know...no one ever reads those lengthy disclaimers and I understand the temptation to ignore reading it, but I discourage you from doing so. If you apply by phone, be prepared to listen for 10-15 minutes while they read it to you in its entirety.

HELP US HELP YOU

We are working together. This is not an "Us vs. Them" type of issue here! The goal of our meeting is to help me to help you with the mindset of quickly and effectively determining your needs, understanding what sort of assistance you qualify for and then getting that assistance to you as fast as possible. Help them do it.

Also, be prepared to repeat all of your information at a later time and provide the same information more than once. That's just the way it is!

Here is a short synopsis of what you can expect during the 30-minute approximate stay of a FEMA inspector:

After you verify the inspector's badge and let him/her into your home, they will ask where the parties can sit down to go over some questions, address the paperwork and ask you to sign the form on the computer screen. At this time, the actual inspection will begin. You'll need to accompany the inspector throughout every single room in the home, including the basement. The inspector will assess all of your real property and personal property. Next comes the exterior inspection. If you have these items, make sure the inspector looks at the crawl space, the air conditioner unit and checks the septic tank and drain field along with any outbuildings that were damaged.

Make sure five (5) photos (the maximum allowed) are taken of the worst damage.

REMEMBER: This inspection is streamlined to address all of your ESSENTIAL NEEDS only.

Now we'll get into the nuts and bolts of the process. The following pages go into more detail of each stage of the inspection.

THE MOST IMPORTANT THING YOU CAN DO IS ANSWER YOUR PHONE!

We do a lot of calling each night, and the first people we contact are the first to get an appointment. It doesn't matter who was the first person to apply. If you don't answer our calls and that other person does, they get that first appointment available. From the moment you call FEMA or go online and submit your application, there is roughly 120 hours for the inspector to get the inspection scheduled, completed and submitted to FEMA. If after three days of calling we can't get in touch with you, the inspection is returned back to FEMA as a "No Contact."

ALWAYS TAKE OUR CALL. If you submit your forms on a Monday but cannot get to your home until the following Thursday, just tell us. The inspector will let FEMA know that the two of you are working together to get the inspection done. This allows your file to remain active on the inspector's computer pad. FEMA just needs to know that an appointment has been made.

If you ignore our call for two or three days, it becomes a "no contact" and we send it back to the host. You will not hear from the inspector again until either you call us back or someone at the host calls you. The host will be persistent in trying to contact you.

If you want to be at the top of the list of inspections, all it takes is for you to be the first to answer your phone and book the inspection! When you book a time for the inspection, be sure that you or someone over the age of 18 who lives there *is there* at the property. Take the time to walk with the inspector through every single room of the home.

If you have Caller ID, remember that most inspectors have their own phones and are probably from out of state, so an unfamiliar number will be calling. In the days after you have applied to FEMA for an inspection, assume that the out-of-state number calling three to five times in one day is the CFI trying to book the inspection that you asked for!

If we have not yet spoken to you but left a message, please listen to that message in its entirety. We take the time to give you a ton of information in those few moments and it's time consuming for us to have to repeat it again. That message itemizes the documents needed and all of the other information required.

LISTEN. When you answer the phone and know it is your CFI calling, let the inspector do the talking. I know it is tough, especially if you are in a desperate situation, but just listen.

"Courage is what it takes to stand up and speak. Courage is also what it takes to sit down and listen." ~Winston Churchill

The average amount of time it takes for the entire call is roughly two minutes. More experienced inspectors can tell you what you need to know in approximately one minute, but only if the applicant is not interrupting or asking questions. The inspector will answer all of your questions *at the inspection.*

Be aware that no dedicated CFI is ever indifferent to the plight of victims. We are not trying to dismiss you or ignore your questions. But the day that you speak with a CFI on the phone is the time and place for only two things: *Listening and Booking Your Inspection.*

Advise the inspector of detours, washed out roads, etc. We are typically not from your area and may not be aware of any impediments reaching your home. If you know that something has happened which will make it difficult for us to get to your house via traditional routes, let the inspector know.

Don't hold off on doing any repairs or recovery work in the days or weeks after the storm. Just be absolutely certain to document every single detail as much as humanly possible and to save the receipts. A good CFI can work with you and your videos or photos to ensure your inspection is fair and accurate - even if you have returned your home and property to pre-disaster conditions.

FRECKS SMART TIP DURING FLOODS

If you're thinking about driving into a flooded street or roadway, think twice. "Turn around. Don't drown!"

RESPECT THE PEOPLE AND THE PROCESS

Advise the inspector if you are delayed or if scheduling conflicts develop. If you book an inspection but are running late or unable to make it, don't ignore us. Give us a call and let us know what's going on. CFIs have a long line of people waiting for them every day. That inspector may have another inspection a block away and still be able to tackle yours afterward.

We know that sometimes people have difficult and lengthy drives to arrive at the property on time after a disaster. Don't force us to head to your home, leave a notice that you were not there, call you and then rebook the whole thing. If you stepped out at the wrong moment and the CFI has left a "Where were you?" note, it will clearly have their phone number listed. In this case, you should call right away. The CFI might still be in the neighborhood doing another inspection and can come back to do yours.

Allow the inspector to focus on his or her work during your brief time together. By following a very fixed and rigid list of steps, they are far less likely to overlook anything, which means that you will get the best results.

Let the CFI have control and wait for them to offer you the chance to ask questions. It is perfectly acceptable to say, "Before we leave this room, did you see that?" Show them your concern. No good CFI will balk at information from an applicant and instead, will appreciate it.

READ THE HELLO LETTER. I give one to each applicant right after I introduce myself and show them my badge. It answers a lot of your questions.

DON'T WORRY ABOUT THE NEIGHBORS GETTING MORE THAN YOU; JUST WORRY ABOUT THEM GETTING WHAT THEY NEED. Avoid making comments to the CFI about what a neighbor received from FEMA. Don't worry about your neighbor's inspection; it has no place in your inspection. Every home is different and every single applicant is going to have a specific set of criteria that determines whether they are eligible for assistance and how much they're qualified to receive. You've probably heard that old phrase of "Keeping up with the Joneses". You have to toss that out the window when you think about your FEMA inspection. There are no Joneses here.

Regardless of what your neighbor told you, it's not likely to bump up any assistance you are qualified to receive. There is no magic formula. There are only the damages done, the losses sustained and the different issues that would allow you to qualify or not. In my years of doing inspections, I have ended up handling entire neighborhoods with similar damages, yet so many different factors went into FEMA's determinations that I'm positive none of the homeowners received matching amounts.

BE HONEST; DON'T COMMIT FRAUD. Lying, exaggerating, bribing and propositioning is punishable by law and very unattractive. In 25 years, I haven't worked a single disaster where at least one applicant didn't try to fool or con me into something. It ranges from the painfully obvious, such as a homeowner who insists they had three feet of flooding when the water line is at an obvious three inches.

Disrespecting inspectors by attempting to make fraudulent claims, false claims of power surges, loss of clothing, etc. will not usually get by them. While they cannot often do anything about misrepresentations, remember that you have just tainted the rest of your inspection with a cloud of doubt in their mind. The CFI will remain watchful about anything else you may show or say to them, and this can lead them to start questioning each issue.

DON'T YELL OR MISTREAT THE INSPECTOR ON THE PHONE OR IN PERSON. CFIs are subcontracted to a large contractor, the company directly aligned with FEMA. We are like the worker bees, and if you get angry, annoyed or hostile with us about the process (or your frustration with it), you are wasting emotion and breath. We cannot do a thing to change any part of the process. The inspector controls only their own performance. They are always hoping that you will work with them as a teammate to get the assistance you qualify for and need. Think of the inspector as a walking data collection device. Try to use the golden rule here and treat that inspector as you would want to be treated if the situation were reversed. Yes, a lot of people have complaints about the government or its agencies, but an inspector can't change circumstances you don't agree with. Always remember that you called them to come out and do this job. No one should be treated unpleasantly. Help us help you!

YOU LOOT, WE SHOOT!

I see this phrase on many homes after a disaster. Don't go to this extreme, but if you witness looting, call the police, the National Guard, FEMA, the fire department - someone! If your belongings were being stolen, remember the Golden Rule to "do unto others as you would have them do unto you." Just remember that this only applies if it doesn't put you in harm's way.

KNOW WHAT TO EXPECT DURING THE PROCESS. Competent, cordial and appropriately-dressed professional inspectors who are independent contractors for FEMA are what you can expect. They contact you by phone within 72 hours (this can change to five days) of your initial application to FEMA with a brief call to set up your inspection at a mutually convenient time.

An inspector should arrive promptly to your appointment and introduce him or herself formally with a photo ID badge and inspector number. Make sure your inspector shows you the ID with their name and inspector number on it.

Take time to ensure that this person is legitimate before allowing them to enter your home. Read their credentials and make note of their ID number. Today's IDs are issued by the Department of Homeland Security (DHS) and look very official (and contain a microchip inside). They will ask you if there's a kitchen table or someplace else to sit down and begin the paperwork.

Take the Hello Letter with you to reference during the walk-through and note the phone numbers shown to call with any follow-up questions. The Hello Letter should have the inspector's name and badge number printed somewhere on it.

An inspection involves a walk-through accompanied at all times by a household member over the age of 18 throughout the entire property. If someone doesn't want to let an inspector enter a room, that is their choice, but it does have to be noted on the inspection report and may impact the outcome.

To assist in precise measuring and documenting damages, the inspector will probably carry a clipboard, computer device, a camera (which may be built into the computer) and a measuring tool. The latter looks like a “Star Trek” gadget that is simply a laser-guided measuring tape, though some CFIs still use the classic metal wheel ones. Laser-guided measuring tapes allow us to point to a wall for an accurate measurement of the distance between that wall and where the inspector is standing. Don’t accept a “guess” at the water line if you have flood damage. Inspectors should be well equipped to portray this damage including measuring the square footage of your home and outside as well.

SIGN THE DOCUMENTS. The signing of documents serves to protect you, the inspector and the agency. It is identical to the way you sign for any UPS or FedEx delivery and is done at the beginning of an inspection via the computer device.

An inspector who will be direct, focused and targeted during the inspection is likely to defer your questions until the end of the inspection. Please don't be offended by this. When an inspector arrives at a home, they tend to want to do the best they can for you, but they want to help everyone else on their list that day too. The main goals of CFIs are to ensure that applicants understand everything about the process and are certain they've covered everything with you. After the inspection, if you still have any unanswered questions, just call FEMA at 800-621-3362.

KNOW THE LIMITS OF THE INSPECTOR’S ABILITIES. Inspectors are prohibited from moving furniture and from climbing on top of houses or under them. If you want the CFI to see something that is behind a lot of boxes or debris, you will have to do all of the moving and clearing. A lot of us joke that we are neither snakes that slither on the ground nor birds that fly up to the roof! It all comes down to liability. FEMA doesn’t want to see applicants ending up liable for an inspector being harmed or vice versa. The inspector will usually crouch down outside of an opening and place their camera into the crawl space. Some use a selfie stick to get pictures further into the opening. Using the flash illuminates the space more than simply slithering around on your belly with a flashlight. We will see damaged duct work, downed insulation and other such problems more effectively.

NOTE: The inspector doesn’t know how much money you will receive or other specifics regarding FEMA’s formula for obtaining assistance. They are not trained in computing this information.

LISTEN MORE THAN YOU SPEAK. Pay 100% attention and act in concert WITH your inspector in order to assure that your needs are being understood by FEMA. Know that we do not see disaster victims in terms of dollar signs. Though you’re hurting from the effects of the disaster and some do try to offer comfort, we cannot view this meeting as a social call. It cannot dissolve into one, no matter how friendly or chatty you tend to be.

As you walk around with the inspector inside and out, just keep your list of "must see" items on hand and only ask questions or point out things if you feel he or she has missed something.

EXPECT TO BE ASKED ABOUT HABITABILITY. The habitability question is: "Have you moved or are you going to move while the repairs are being made?" If you answer "yes" and you are eligible, you may receive housing assistance depending on FEMA's decision after they review your inspection details. If you answer "no", you might not receive any housing assistance depending on FEMA's after-review decision. Ultimately, the inspector must determine if your house is safe, secure and sanitary enough to live in (habitable).

At the end of the entire inspection process, all inspectors should encourage you to ask them any remaining questions you may have. I begin to close out an inspection with, "Do you have any other questions or anything we need to discuss?" If an inspector doesn't ask you for questions, you are well within your rights to stop them in their tracks and ask.

TIME IS OF THE ESSENCE! We devote so much attention to taking charge and monitoring time because other disaster victims are waiting for our help. If you are unprepared, full of unnecessary questions and complaints or late for your appointment without notifying the inspector, we get upset because it's wildly unfair for other disaster victims. Never be offended or put off by a take-charge inspector. That person has your back, but they also have the back of everyone else they need to see that day and the next, and usually for many days after.

SOME THINGS TO BE AWARE OF (RED FLAGS)

- **Incompetent or impaired inspectors:** You have the right to ask the inspector at your door about his or her experience and length of time on the job as well as report any inspector whose behavior is unacceptable to you. No inspector worth their name will arrive without gear. If they try to do the work without such essentials as the computer, Hello Letter, measuring devices and a camera for photos, you'll know there's a problem. If this happens, make sure to get their name and badge number because you'll probably need to call in a complaint.
- **Inexperienced inspectors:** On a major disaster, subcontractors use their best inspectors for training, QC (Quality Control) and appeal work. They pull in new inspectors through recruitment. In the old days, this wasn't ideal because an inspector could be almost anyone off the street. Today, a candidate who has completely valid credentials but who might have had a foreclosure, bankruptcy or other financial glitch on their record is automatically disqualified from being a CFI. Regardless of this higher level of security, some CFIs might be a new recruit. The recruit is in a training environment for one day, then receives one day of field work alongside a seasoned inspector and may have to share that experience with a handful of other inexperienced inspectors. They are reviewed for a

few days, then released on their own and assigned to heavily-damaged areas with little or no experience three or four days later. You, as an applicant, aren't aware of this which means you won't necessarily know whether or not you're getting a solid inspection. On a positive note, remember that all inspectors today, whether new or seasoned, have had extensive FBI/DHS background checks.

I encourage you to ask a few questions about your inspector's disaster background. For instance, "Have you done tornado work in the past?" or "How long have you been inspecting?" You have every right to know the truth about your CFI and it is up to you to figure out whether or not they're doing the best job possible. One major contractor had trained more than 90,000 CFIs, and yet when Hurricane Sandy devastated New York and New Jersey, only 3,000 showed up. The high turnover rate for CFIs is a problem, and in the wake of each disaster, inexperienced inspectors have to be trained to handle the inspections. A lot of those inspections done after Hurricane Sandy could have been substandard and may be valid candidates for appeal by the applicants. There's no hard numbers out there that identifies how many of those applications were appealed, but I doubt it was anywhere near the number that could have easily been challenged. We count on the appeal process, as well as Quality Control inspections done periodically, to shine a light on anything that might have slipped through the cracks with a less experienced inspector.

- **Kitchen Table Inspections:** When the inspector is in your home for five or ten minutes and sits only at the kitchen table or in some other room, never physically inspecting every room in the house, this is called a *kitchen table inspection*. You don't want this to happen. Yes, it is fast and convenient, but it hardly gives you the fair treatment you deserve. Know your rights. If your inspection is over before you know it and you feel like you're standing there with your head spinning because so many things were missed, CALL and ask for a re-inspection (see below on how to do this).
- **Fake Inspectors:** Call the police immediately if someone shows up claiming to be a FEMA inspector wanting to do an inspection but you have not yet applied, or if they don't possess an official FEMA/DHS badge. FEMA hats and shirts are NOT signs of an official inspector. I've heard many stories of con artists knocking on doors wearing FEMA hats, t-shirts or other gear with a FEMA logo claiming to offer inspections. They may even ask for money to do these inspections or use this chance to scope out your home. Unless you have called for the inspection, don't let anyone inside. Check out their clothing. If it's too nice or too shoddy, this could likely mean they're not CFIs. Fake inspectors tend to work for around two weeks in their chosen area and then they have to get out of town because law enforcement agencies become aware of them. However, while they work their nasty scams, they bilk hundreds of victims out of a lot of money. Some inspectors may do "cold calls" and show up without successfully

making an appointment first, but inspectors don't solicit work on a *door-to-door* basis. That person standing there with a FEMA hat saying he or she is there to do an inspection is not who they say they are. Plus, the latest guidelines from FEMA prohibits CFI inspectors from wearing any type of FEMA logo.

NOTE: FEMA *employees* are allowed to wear FEMA logo shirts, hats and jackets, but employees do not perform inspections.

At such times, close the door and call the police. Don't confront them or try to get their license plate if it means stepping outside of your home. Give the police as accurate of a description as possible. Also, call FEMA's 800 number and tell them.

REMEMBER! FEMA itself does go door-to-door on disasters handing out flyers and urging victims to apply, but it does not do the inspections at such times. They won't knock on the door, hand you a flyer and ask you to do an inspection right then and there. You'll get contacted ONLY after you call and apply.

- **Fee based services:** There has never been and will hopefully never be any fee based services for disaster victims who seek FEMA inspections. We never charge any fees to come out and inspect or re-inspect. Anyone who tries to charge you is committing fraud.
- **Fake or untrustworthy contractors:** Unfortunately, during disasters, criminals looking to defraud victims come out of the woodwork. Be very careful, check references and licenses. Get contracts before paying anyone for any work. What happens most is criminals circle around to different neighborhoods and they might even have nicely printed cards that advertise they're working the entire area. They might even extend special prices for roofing, cleanup, etc. The scam here is that they respond to every single call they receive with a demand for a hefty down payment because "the response is so big." They will take your money and even give you some sort of contract. The whole thing is a fraud though and this "firm" is likely to be gone in a matter of a few weeks.

Unless you have checked out references, called the Better Business Bureau and performed due diligence on companies similar to the scams listed above, do not give them a dime. Check their licensing and insurance. Ask other neighbors if they've hired them and their results. It's a good idea to always get three to five different bids for work. Don't necessarily take the first one or the least expensive one.

Trustworthy groups do exist and try to help people recover quickly by heading out when things are still pretty chaotic. These are the people you often see doing the initial cleanup and repairs, but it is up to you to distinguish between the liars and the cheats from the hard working and honest firms.

Report Price Gouging

Taking advantage of disaster victims by price gouging is a punishable crime that can carry fines, jail time or both. Immediately report any price gouging practices to the authorities. This especially applies to the elderly population who sometimes can become targets.

TEMPTATION. I talked about this already in regards to not attempting to "pull one over" on your inspector. Don't think you will get more money from FEMA by exaggerating the extent of your damages or by "working a deal" with the CFI. Frauds from Hurricanes Katrina and Rita totaled more than one billion dollars. Even with the established penalties being $250,000 in fines, time in jail or both, fraudsters took and still take chances. Because of the enormity of fraud in those hurricanes, the National Center for Disaster Fraud was started. This group relentlessly pursues open cases and it may take them years to find people, but anyone who makes a fraudulent claim will be pursued to the greatest extent possible. You may not even know you've been discovered until you file your annual income tax and receive a letter informing you that all future tax refunds are now being withheld because of the fraudulent disaster claim.

If you use FEMA funds for something other than essentials and FEMA finds out, that too can trigger a request for repayment. I once discovered that someone used a FEMA check to have a diamond embedded in their front tooth. I also know of people who took luxury vacations, bought expensive cars and others who went gambling. Using these funds for nonessential needs can prompt FEMA to request the return of every single red penny and more.

To avoid being scrutinized by FEMA for fraud, remember that *by your signature* you are certifying that: 1.) Only one application has been submitted for my household; 2.) All information provided regarding my application for FEMA disaster assistance is true and correct to the best of my knowledge; and, 3.) I will RETURN any disaster aid money I received from FEMA or the State if I receive insurance or other money for the same loss, or if I do not use the FEMA disaster aid money for the purpose for which it was intended."[14]

Do the right thing. This is not government money fraudsters we're talking about here, folks. It's taxpayer dollars being stolen. Do the right thing and call 800-323-8603 or send an email regarding your complaint directly to this address: DHSOIGHOTLINE@DHS.gov if you know of someone led into temptation.

FOLLOW THROUGH. I'm confident in providing the following information to you on what to expect from your inspector when the actual inspection day arrives.

If the inspector is showing signs of doing their job poorly, you need to consider just how poorly they are doing it and whether or not you want them to continue. You don't have to work with someone if you feel they are behaving in a questionable manner or just aren't doing the job properly. Be courteous about it, ask them to end the inspection and get in touch with FEMA right away. You can persist and try to work with them to get the best results, but if someone seems very unprofessional or inexperienced...well, you might just be out of luck with this person. Your next best step might be to let the inspector finish the job, do the inspection, then call FEMA to file a complaint.

Likewise, if you receive the results of your inspection and don't believe everything was considered accurately, you can appeal by writing a letter to FEMA telling them you want to appeal your original inspection. In the old days, all this took was a phone call to FEMA. Things have changed a bit, and instead of verbally explaining things over the phone, you'll have to draft a brief paragraph explaining precisely why you're appealing.

REMEMBER: You only have 60 days after you receive your letter to do so.

The appeal process will result in a new inspector coming to your home and looking at everything that was done in the first inspection. This will be a CFI from the same firm, but most likely someone with more experience or who is exceptional at quality control, or possibly someone who is a supervisor. Regardless, appeals get a seasoned inspector to the site.

Complaining about the performance of the first inspector or the overall outcome of the report will not penalize you. The new CFI is not out there to punish you for making a second-look request. Feel confident and secure in using the fraud lines or appeal process to make things right. Taking money out of your hands or out of the hands of other disaster victims who deserve it is not anyone's mission. Filing an appeal to have a second-look request shouldn't bother any inspector. It's your right.

NOTE: You can use all of the same videos and images to show to the second inspector who arrives for the appeal inspection and hopefully alter the outcome of an unsatisfactory report.

Essential needs are not the same as reimbursement for losses and that is truly the major distinguishing point between FEMA and insurance firms. FEMA will not replace your $3,000 television. That would fall under an insurance issue, and if your insurance covers that loss, it is unlikely you would get any funds for that same television from FEMA. FEMA looks at your homeowners insurance policy as part of its calculations. It looks at what you are going to receive and will not "double up" on payments. Be clear that you understand everything about your insurance company before you pick up that phone to appeal. If you do see that there are issues and items that have been overlooked by the CFI *and* they are not things that will be covered by any insurance policy, definitely appeal.

SOME MAJOR THINGS TO REMEMBER

1. Don't remove a single thing until you photo document everything.
2. Receipts! Receipts! Receipts! for Insurance, FEMA and the IRS.
3. Appeal, Appeal, Appeal! Don't stop until you're satisfied.
4. No flood insurance? Apply for FEMA; get an SBA loan to rebuild.
5. Once you have lived through a disaster, be prepared for the next one which might occur sooner than you think as in the case of strong earthquake aftershocks. Learn from the first one. Know the supplies you need.
6. Beat the rush and evacuate early so you don't have to suffer in an expensive dive motel!

UPDATE 2015

What happens when there is no FEMA, such as in the Kobe, Japan earthquake? This is slowly happening in America. While writing this book, three disasters were being considered for a disaster declaration, yet it hadn't happened. Why?

Let's look at Michigan. It had extreme flooding in the summer of 2014 with estimates in the hundreds of millions of dollars for damages. The figures also point to over 100,000 people who will apply for FEMA. The affected area may get a public infrastructure declaration, but not for individual assistance because the state then has to pay 25% of the total price tag. Most states do not have any money these days, therefore, the disaster still hadn't been declared for individual assistance, known as IHP (Individual Household Program). The same held true for Hawaii after Hurricane Iselle hit Hilo on the big island in 2014. As of this writing, those regions remain without individual disaster assistance declarations but some did receive public funds to rebuild roads, etc.

This also held true after the recent Napa earthquake. Many people had earthquake insurance there, but most of those policies had such high deductibles that no one could afford to pay them to the insurance companies; therefore, no claims were issued. In addition, a lot of the homeowners didn't have enough damage to meet the deductible.

In one example, a Napa homeowner had $5,000 dollars in damages, but the insurance policy deductible was $10,000. The policy only covered 50% of structure and 50% of contents. That turned out to be a "No Claim" decision with the insurance company winning on that one. The homeowner is now out $5,000 for repairs to his home.

Unfortunately, being insured is still your best and only decision when attempting to cover yourself against losses. More and more states have less than the money needed to ask for a disaster declaration from the federal government or FEMA. On a personal level, more proof to me is that I haven't been out on a disaster since Hurricane Sandy. Sure, I could have gone out on three different ones during that time, but it wasn't economically feasible for me to work on them - and the FEMA inspectors who did go lost their shirts financially TRYING TO HELP PEOPLE.

The reason I started writing above about the Kobe Japan earthquake was to point out when homeowners there didn't have earthquake insurance and their homes were more than 50% percent damaged, those homes were bulldozed into rubble and hauled off at the homeowners' expense.

This could happen right here in good old America. Think about it. Where would you go? How would you live? Your home is gone. Maybe you are elderly and don't have the resources, little or no income or are on a fixed income such

MICHIGAN FLOODS

If you know anyone in Michigan who experienced flooding and received a denial letter from FEMA for assistance, they should file an appeal NO LATER than 60 days from the date on the denial letter. There are many reasons why they could have been denied, including inexperienced inspectors, software glitches, bad documentation, maybe they were unable to prove occupancy or ownership, duplicate applications, and so on. A lot of people just give up at this point. Don't let this happen to your friends or family! Go to http://www.fema.gov/help-after-disaster and find out exactly how to appeal. Good luck!

as SSI – and NO FEMA! There are thousands of elderly victims in Japan who still don't have a home or permanent place to live because either they didn't have insurance at all or didn't have the right kind of insurance.

It's only a matter of time before this is commonplace here in America. The same thing already happened during Hurricane Sandy in the Seaside Heights area. The elderly there had bought their homes years ago and paid them off, but many didn't carry flood insurance. Hurricane Sandy came along and destroyed their homes.

Now where do they go? What do they do? They can't qualify for a SBA loan to rebuild. They had no insurance, and even if they had been able to get the full amount of assistance from FEMA, it would have been a maximum of approximately $30,000 and a possible maximum of eighteen months housing assistance. WHAT THEN? The money and housing assistance always runs out quickly when you're displaced, which happened to many Hurricane Sandy victims.

I know that insurance costs money that a lot of people don't have, but still - insurance isn't just the best answer in today's world. It is the only answer.

MY OWN DISASTER STORY
The Storm

On February 6, 2015, a big storm hit California and Nevada packing winds gusts from 85 to 140 mph. From Reno to Gardnerville and beyond, the storm wreaked havoc. The damaging winds were too much for the area and whole neighborhoods were affected. Most of the damage occurred to roofs, fences and trees. It was unbelievable what a little wind gust could do, not to mention the ignorance of friends and neighbors who wouldn't take my advice and called their insurance companies about their damages.

I had a book signing scheduled the next day and Reno's Channel 4 news team was coming out to interview me.[15] The news team came early so they could broadcast this valuable information to prevent people from making a big mistake, thereby determining their damages first before calling the insurance companies.

First and foremost, and I'm stressing this again, if you don't have enough damages to meet your deductible at two to three times over that amount, you don't want to call them. What you will end up with is a No Claim because you don't have enough damage. That is two strikes against you – one, for alerting them; two, for the No Claim, putting you at risk. I actually called my own insurance agent to ask if other clients had called in for adjusters to assess their damages. To my astonishment, the insurance company had been advising them not to request a storm adjuster because more than likely, their damages wouldn't meet their deductibles. Many ignored this advice and were issued No Claim letters. Doing this puts you on their radar like thousands of others during Hurricane Sandy.

Let's take just one example from my many neighbors who didn't listen to this advice and found out the hard way. Here's how it all played out.

Betsy had over 80 feet of fence blown down, 30 or 40 asphalt shingles blown off the roof and a large tree uprooted, now leaning up against her house. After depreciation, her insurance company offered $250 for her 20 year-old fence, $150 to replace her 25 year-old roof shingles and zero for the tree leaning against her house because the policy didn't include anything for landscaping issues.

NOTE: Most policies don't include landscaping issues.

She needed a professional to remove the tree. They would give her $100 for debris clean-up. The adjuster's figures totaled $500 dollars. Her policy had a $1,000 deductible, meaning she would have to pay that to the insurance company *before* they would pay anything. The $500 amount was way short of her deductible.

She received a No Claim and so did thousands of other people. The insurance companies made out like bandits not having to pay on thousands of claims because deductibles were not met. Sure, there were some homes that had more damage, went over the deductible and had legitimate claims, but at what cost?

BE FRECKS SMART. Don't call the insurance company unless damage is two to three times higher than your deductible. It's simply not worth it. Save that call for when you really need it and have major damage.

Here's my story on the same storm. I had three sections of fence blown down, about 10 shingles blown off the roof and one tree uprooted laying on the ground which didn't damage anything.

I knew I didn't have a claim at all. My fence was over 20 years old, I repaired the roof myself and for the tree, I got out the chainsaw and cut it up into firewood.

Our power was out for two days. How did I survive? I mention on my website how to live comfortably during a disaster.[16] I took my solar powered lights out of the yard and used them for lights inside the house. I had previously changed my electric stove to gas so I could cook with no effort if my power went out, plus I'd changed my hot water heater to gas at the same time (You can always use your barbeque to cook meals on as well).

I charged up extra batteries in my car along with my computer and a few other items. I barbequed a steak, had a glass of wine and watched a movie on my computer while hundreds of other people sat miserable in the dark. After everything was cleaned up and all damages fixed, I was out $27.

Even more happier? I didn't have a No Claim with my insurance company like many others now do.

NOTE: Your car can be a lifesaver and help you to live in more comfortable conditions during a disaster. Keep it well ventilated if you're running it to charge things. Don't sleep in it while it's running either!

THE DREAM IS OVER!!!

Bob and Sally worked hard all of their lives to make their dreams come true. They retired at 50 and bought their dream home on the Jersey Shore. They paid cash and had no mortgage payment of any kind. They also bought the necessary basic homeowners insurance - fire and theft.

Well, sometimes dreams can become nightmares. Along came a hurricane named Irene. Luckily for Bob and Sally, the eye of the storm hit 60 miles away and they only sustained minor damages to their new home. A few shingles, a little siding, a few minor roof leaks left very small stains in the ceiling drywall and some debris to clean up in their yard. For the most part, they dodged the bullet as did many, many others.

Over the next few months, they were solicited several times by different insurance companies to buy flood insurance. They talked about it and decided not to purchase it for several reasons. It was a little expensive, they owned their home so the bank/mortgage company didn't make them buy it and they were on fixed incomes by then. They had some money put away for minor repairs if another disaster came knocking and were pretty confident they didn't need flood insurance.

Like so many other people thought in that area, they had dodged the big hurricane and felt safe that the odds of another hurricane hitting were low and wouldn't happen for many years. Before Irene hit, the area hadn't seen a hurricane in 62 years.

The next year, another storm of the century hit the Jersey Shore. This time, it was really bad. Hurricane Sandy roared in with a vengeance and caused billions of dollars in damage there and in adjoining New York.

From my perspective, the devastation was some of the worst I'd ever seen. The flooding was enormous, the evacuation was massive and up to five feet of sand had washed up into Bob and Sally's town, burying the streets. The boardwalk in the area was torn from its piers and did even more damage smashing homes apart, setting some homes adrift into the ocean. Many were ripped from their foundations and destroyed with only the concrete foundation left standing, which many people witnessed watching live news footage of this mega disaster.

Bob and Sally were forced to evacuate the area and for almost four weeks, they didn't know what, if anything, had happened to their dream home. During this time, the Army Corp of Engineers, first responders, National Guard and cleaning crews had the job of clearing debris and the miles of sand that stood five feet high.

All they could do was wait for word. After it was safer to enter, FEMA started a bus trip lottery system to taxi homeowners into the shore area to grab as much of their belongings as they could carry out (if their homes were still intact and not red tagged), so Bob and Sally asked other neighborhood members allowed to go in if they had seen their home. No one was able to give them any good or bad news, or perhaps they just didn't want to tell them the bad news.

They even tried to catch glimpses of their house on TV news coverage from helicopters, but to no avail. Finally, the day Bob and Sally feared came. It was their turn to take the bus ride over to survey their home and grab some belongings. I can't image what they must have felt like during that ride over, hoping for the best, thinking positive and praying the storm's hand had passed over their home, but all the while knowing so many others had been destroyed.

They had already called FEMA and applied as instructed by their insurance company. Why? The insurance company already knew that they weren't able to do much for them because they didn't have flood insurance.

That day, they would meet their assigned FEMA inspector where their home used to be (which GPS helped to locate). It was devastating for the inspector to see the anguish, total shock and overwhelming sickness Bob and Sally felt. Only foundations were left on most of their street. The thousand yard stare developed in Bob and Sally – a phenomenon I see happening to people who experience or witness devastation – trying to wrap their minds around what had occurred and how to cope with it.

The FEMA inspector had to ask, "Which foundation is yours?"

"That one," Bob replied, gesturing, "and that's our second floor over there." He pointed two blocks away where it had been red tagged, DO NOT ENTER. They couldn't even go inside to get any of their belongings. Because they had evacuated when the disaster first hit as they were directed to do, they had managed to save some of their most prized personal possessions...a few car loads, but that was it.

Bob and Sally only had two hours to grab what they could find laying around and carry it back with them on the bus to their hotel. As a FEMA inspector, these are gut-wrenching situations where you want to do all you can for victims. You want to give them help, hope and comfort which is extremely hard when you can't provide the answers they so desperately need.

WHERE IN THE HELL DO WE GO FROM HERE???

For Bob and Sally, it was horrible. Here's what they were looking at. Their dream house had been completely destroyed. With no flood insurance, their homeowners policy was going to do very little for them. They had applied for FEMA and could possibly receive a grant for up to $30,000 dollars. They could possibly have been offered an SBA loan package with the low interest rate, but both were retired and on fixed incomes. Most likely, they wouldn't have qualified. Very few resources were available for them.

The ride back to the hotel was one I would never want to experience. And back at the hotel, matters got even worse.

Later that day, after their visit to the shore, Sally went to the store to buy some steaks and a bottle of wine in order for her and Bob to at least have a nice meal and talk about making plans about where to go from here. While Sally was gone, Bob committed suicide.

No matter how tough, smart, well-rounded, adaptable or able to overcome bad situations some people are, the sheer magnitude of what happened can just be way too much to handle. I have seen it over and over again during disasters. Some take the easy way out and simply give up or they run off. Others man up, see things through, conquer and overcome all of the adversities life just handed them. Others do the most devastating thing of all...they check out and leave their loved ones to handle the nightmare – the disaster that follows the disaster, all alone.

I have cried many man tears about situations I've witnessed firsthand, and I'm pretty sure I don't need to explain to you anymore about being prepared. Insurance isn't the best answer. It is the only answer, but *only* if it's the right kind of insurance.

Save your life. Save who you love. Save your home. Save what you love. Save your DREAM!!

WHAT'S HAPPENING AT FEMA TODAY

With all my continuing training and education, with new FEMA guidelines,

BE FRECKS SMART!

Among the horrific disaster stories in *Dust in the Wind*, you'll learn how one compromised house can take out an entire neighborhood, especially during a hurricane.

When the authorities tell you to evacuate – evacuate! Ask anyone who didn't evacuate and lived to tell about it, especially those who ended up being forced to move to an emergency shelter. They will never live like that again.

There's good reason not to play with Mother Nature. Watch firsthand disaster footage of Hurricane Sandy and view photos of its wrath on my websites:
http://www.dustinthewindFEMAbook.com or
http://www.Celebrities4DisasterRelief.org.

updates and changes to the new Automated Construction Estimating (ACE4) software that includes individual assistance (IHP) changes where stricter guidelines now exist, I've come to the conclusion that this year FEMA will be paying out less than ever before on disaster specific damages to real and personal property. It's almost to the point of why even apply and putting yourself through the red tape, aggravation, torment and scrutiny of a few dollars to help you recover. The bottom line is, if you don't have insurance and the right coverage, where else are you going to turn?

Additionally, it's getting harder for experienced FEMA inspectors to show up on disaster sites. Here's what's happening on the FEMA inspector side of things.

On any large scale disaster, the two contractors that all of the inspectors work for bring everyone in their cadre. If they don't meet the number of inspectors requested by FEMA, the contractors train new inspectors on site. This has been going on for years. It used to be so bad that they hired people right off the street. If you could breathe, you could do FEMA inspections. As mentioned before, one contractor trained over 90,000 inspectors during a 17-year period, yet on Hurricane Sandy, they couldn't get 3,000 inspectors to show up.

The contractors are under the gun with FEMA. In their contracts, it stipulates that 20,000 inspections per day need to be performed within two weeks of deployment. *It's never been done in my 25 years as an inspector.*

Twice, the contractors got close. Once after four months of doing inspections and training new inspectors on site, 16,000 inspections were done in one day. The second time, 19,000 were done in a day after three months of filling the disaster area with inexperienced inspectors in an attempt to reach that magic number. Once the workload diminishes, inspectors start getting sent home.

Here is the real problem. Thousands of inexperienced inspectors get deployed on a large scale disaster only to be sent home after a week to 10 days. Sure, they get trained, reviewed and get some work done (usually 10 inspections in a week), but they never really learn how to do a good inspection. The real purpose for inexperienced inspectors to work during disasters is to fill up the contractors' computers with inspections. This gets FEMA off their back with all of the work out in the field. This, unfortunately, means that for the most part, inspections aren't being processed by those most knowledgeable in the field.

What do inexperienced FEMA inspectors hear from their bosses? Something like, "We know you didn't make any money on this disaster, but we'll make it up to you on the next one." After hearing this "broken record" spiel two or three times, the inspectors just don't show up anymore.

They learn that this is not the best way to make a living. Inspectors must leave their homes and families for indefinite periods of time, still paying their rent or mortgage, car payment, insurance, taxes, kids, plus all of their other bills on top of paying for the usually inflated costs of lodging, rental cars, gas, food and other expenses at the disaster site – in essence, two households and more. But more importantly, under these conditions, it's not the best way to help people on the worst day of their lives.

Let's take a look at the last couple of years of federally declared disasters. Luckily, there hasn't been that many since Hurricane Sandy. The bad news is, more and more inexperienced inspectors aren't getting hands-on training in the field. The turnover rate is unreal.

The following chart shows recent flood disasters and may illustrate why:

State Affected	Year of Occurrence	Inspectors Deployed	Inspectors Sent Home After 7-10 Days
Illinois	2013	500	400
Colorado	2013	186	150
Michigan	2014	600	500
Texas	2015	300	250

How many disaster deployments and getting sent home after a week does it take to realize you're never going to make a living and that you're being used by the corporate machine? Unlike before, contractors now push an hourly wage onto inspectors instead of the previous piecework rate which is similar to what insurance adjusters receive (as previously mentioned, this hourly rate switch is occurring in the insurance field too), so now you have seasoned inspectors leaving the industry too. Who's going to fill these empty but challenging jobs? Your guess is as good as mine.

Because of the large turnover in inexperienced inspectors, on the next large scale disaster, FEMA plans to streamline the inspection process. Instead of itemizing inspection reports, basically all the CFI inspector needs to do is prove primary residence, the occupancy, the number of occupied bedrooms, the square footage of the dwelling, obtain the proper signatures and then determine whether the applicant(s) experienced minor, medium or major damage to the dwelling. The applicant(s) will be awarded funds appropriately. This process has been tried before on two other disasters and did speed up the process, but at whose benefit? It's more general; less specific. If you're not happy with the results, you can still appeal within 60 days from the time you receive your denial or assistance letter. If it's found you received too much, they'll attach your income tax refund with interest to recover their funds.

Many in the industry know this is FEMA's way of covering the two contractors' hindquarters for hiring inexperienced inspectors when the next Katrina, Sandy or other major disaster occurs.

For disaster victims, the reality is hoping to find yourself in a small scale disaster as opposed to a large scale disaster in order to increase your chances of getting a seasoned inspector. But due to FEMA now using the bull's eye approach to deploy (using inspectors from the center of a disaster who live there, *then* working outwards and flying in more experienced inspectors to the disaster area to save on transportation costs), this might no longer be the case.

FEMA and its two contractors will assure you that with all of their online training, seminars, webinars, mobile unit training centers and disaster training houses that all inspectors are well trained to provide good inspections for people.

But as most first responders will tell you, there's truly only one great way to train, and that is with hands-on experience. It's imperative to your financial recovery to have a seasoned inspector/adjuster report on your damages.

Overall, these facts and statistics all boil down to one thing: how does this help the victims of disasters? You may have witnessed some disaster victims wearing t-shirts that say, "What does F.E.M.A. stand for? FIX EVERYTHING MY ASS!"

HURRICANE SANDY

With all of the exploitation that occurred during this tragedy, the saving grace happened with the tens of thousands of individuals, first responders, businesses, volunteers and just neighbors helping neighbors who freely donated their time and resources to the disaster victims.

Special commendation goes out to the New York and New Jersey police and fire departments who went above and beyond their duty to save lives and property.

SECTION THREE

HELPFUL INFO, FORMS AND LISTS BEFORE, DURING AND AFTER A DISASTER

DISASTERS HAPPEN WITHOUT WARNING!

Don't Wait Until the Last Minute to Get Supplies

You all have seen it over and over again on TV. Every year as a hurricane approaches land, tens of thousands of people scramble and flock to the stores to buy supplies. Most will end up with less than they needed because they waited too long. In these situations, the store shelves empty fast.

Be **FRECKS SMART** and save yourself a lot of grief. Why not be prepared and feel relieved from the torment, the frustration of waiting in long lines with hot, sweaty and angry people? Go shopping for your disaster needs beforehand at an easy, leisurely relaxed pace. Sit back at home with a cold beer and watch all the procrastinators on TV fight each other for that last speck of crumbs off the shelves. Shake your head in disbelief at the two annoyed shoppers fighting over the last generator, piece of plywood or tarp, knowing you have everything you need to survive after a disaster.

Instead, you can concentrate on protecting your home and family. Meanwhile, down at the stores, people are slugging it out for that last bottle of water. Since you were prepared, you can decide if you want to evacuate early and not sit in bumper-to-bumper traffic.

Take your supplies and turn this into a mini-vacation or family outing until the storm passes and you can head back home. The bonus here is that you can pick and choose what nice hotel to stay in and not be forced to stay in some dive motel that will charge you an arm and a leg for a room. They *can* and *do* take advantage of evacuees to make a fast buck. For the most part, their motto isn't how can I help people, but how can I make money from this situation. Sad, but true.

New York's Hurricane Sandy is a perfect example of this. Hundreds of FEMA inspectors stayed in Red Cross shelters, tent cities and their cars, just like all the victims. The cheap hotel rooms went for $400 to $500 a night! Be disaster smart; leave early, stay away until the storm passes and enjoy yourself until it's time to head home. Nothing against the Red Cross...it's great to have somewhere to go, but ask anyone who has stayed there for any length of time, or any Katrina victim who stayed in the Superdome. Have you ever slept in a gym with thousands of other people six inches apart? Crying babies, coughing, sickness, talking, laughter when you're trying to sleep, etc. You can do so much better if you're prepared!

Over the years, I have seen hundreds of victims build the ultimate disaster bunker, stocking it up with top-of-the-line everything - from generators, survivor kits, food, water, clothing, beds, etc. WHY? Because they had to stay in a shelter before! They will never live like that again in any disaster, big or small.

It's a good idea to have a disaster plan and disaster supplies year round. Stock up on the items listed on the following pages. Check your supplies regularly to make sure you have enough on hand. If you have an adequate supply, there's no need to rush and purchase them or face shortages when a disaster is about to hit.

STAY INFORMED AND SURVIVE

Before impending disasters, especially during tornado season, emergency alerts can be broadcasted over the weather radio that signal a touchdown, then prove to be false. Maybe the tornado lit on land, then reverted back up into the sky.

Many people get annoyed by the shrill sound of this alert, especially while sleeping. After a few nights of this, they shut their weather radios off.

Don't unplug your weather radio! You may be unplugging your life.

DISASTER PREPARATION, EMERGENCY SUPPLY & TO-DO LIST FOR EVERYDAY SAFETY

- Certified fire extinguisher
- Smoke detector with battery
- Carbon monoxide detector

Before the season starts:

- MAKE A FAMILY PLAN. Who does what, and where will your family ride out the storm.
- Locate your water and gas meters and electrical shutoff.
- Know the disaster plan of your child's school or daycare.
- Trim trees and store loose objects.

- Install/test your smoke detector. Do the same with your carbon monoxide detector. These items save lives, reduce property damage and reduce risk of fires year round but especially in a disaster.
- Use a video camera to tape the contents of your home and store the videotape.
- Be sure that you are properly insured and understand the conditions of your policy. This will save you from unfortunate surprises during recovery.
- Make plans to board your pet if you plan to go to a shelter.
- Obtain cash or travelers checks.
- Establish an out-of-state contact to call in case of emergency.
- Photocopy important papers and store them safely. If you evacuate after a disaster, make sure to take them with you.

KEEP IN A WATERPROOF, FIREPROOF PORTABLE CONTAINER

- Will, insurance policies, contracts, deeds, stocks and bonds
- Passports, social security cards, immunization records
- Bank account numbers
- Credit card account numbers and companies
- Inventory of valuable household goods, important telephone numbers
- Family records (birth, marriage, death certificates)
- If you have difficulty remembering passwords, store a copy of these on a secure online site or in another safe place.

WATER

- Water will be needed for drinking, cooking and bathing. Store enough bottled water for all members of your family and pets before the storm.
- Clean (non-drinking) water that could be used for bathing & washing dishes will often be available in your water heater.
- Before a disaster strikes and the plumbing could get damaged, fill up your bathtub and any other containers you have.

FIRST AID

Dangerous weather conditions can prevent emergency vehicles from responding to emergency situations. Preparing yourself and your family with CPR and First Aid training can save your life!

BE FRECKS SMART ALL YEAR LONG!

Using solar lights when landscaping your yard can provide you with loads of help should a power outage occur after a disaster.

Just leave them in the yard during the day soaking up all of the natural solar energy, then bring them inside in the evening to light your home all night. They will save you money on flashlight batteries and are a whole lot safer than candles too.

POWER

- During a storm, phone and electrical lines may go down. Electrical power can be off for several days after a storm, so plan for power outages.
- Plan ahead for loss of water, power, phone, internet, cable and television. You may want to have other activities on hand for your family such as board games, card games, books and crafts.

Have your emergency food and supplies ready and up to date. Use the list on the following pages to plan and shop for supplies in advance.

EMERGENCY SUPPLY KIT SHOPPING LIST

Everyone needs to prepare for emergency situations, but shopping for supplies can be expensive and strenuous. Obtain items a few at a time before an event to reduce the stress of recovery by enabling you to save gas, avoid long lines and the possibility of empty shelves. Check your supplies now to make sure you have adequate food for 5 to 7 days. Also stock up on personal care and cleaning items. Don't forget disposable plates, cups and utensils, paper towels, toilet paper and disposable wipes. If you don’t have extra amounts of these supplies on hand, you should purchase them over a period of weeks as your budget permits.

SUGGESTED FOOD ITEMS

Some disaster guides suggest from one to four each of the following items. Since family sizes vary, you may want to determine how many of each of the food items listed would provide adequate nutrition for your own family for 5 to 7 days. Use and replace perishable food items when they are close to their expiration dates.

- One gallon of water per person per day for at least 5 days, for drinking and sanitation
- Sandwich bread (freeze until needed)
- Boxes of quick energy snacks (i.e. granola bars or raisins)
- Cans of soup (a ready to eat variety is best)
- Top Ramen soup
- Box of crackers
- Boxes of dry cereal
- Canned milk
- Cans of fruit
- Cans of meat or another protein source (tuna, salmon, peanut butter)
- Cans of vegetables
- Jar of jelly or jam
- Large cans of juice
- Instant powdered drinks (coffee, tea, fruit-flavored punch)
- Two packages of eating utensils, paper cups, paper plates
- Can opener

HEALTH AND FIRST AID ITEMS

- Bottle of shampoo
- Box of sanitary hand wipes
- Large tube of toothpaste
- Antiseptic
- Deodorant
- Tweezers
- Facial tissues
- Two rolls of paper towels
- Four rolls of toilet paper

MEDICATION

- Extra supply of prescription medication
- Aspirin and/or acetaminophen
- Antidiarrheal medicine
- Adult vitamins
- Thermometer
- Bandages (assorted sizes), rolls of gauze and first aid tape
- Hydrogen peroxide
- First-Aid book
- Petroleum jelly
- Rubbing alcohol
- Insect repellent

CLEANING ITEMS

- Liquid dish soap
- Pairs of latex gloves
- Broom, mop and bucket
- Unscented liquid bleach

STORAGE ITEMS

- Two boxes of large plastic zip bags
- Plastic wrap
- Two rolls of aluminum foil
- Three boxes heavy-duty garbage bags
- Waterproof portable plastic containers with lids

COMMON TOOLS

- Battery-operated radio and extra batteries or *Red Cross* hand crank radio[17]
- Flashlight and flashlight batteries
- Assorted safety pins, needle & thread
- Scissors
- Screwdrivers, pliers, vise grips
- Hammers
- Heavy work gloves
- Matches
- Stove fuel, charcoal, lighter fluid
- Camping or utility knife
- One box disposable dust masks
- Plastic safety goggles

HEAVY TOOLS

- Plywood and fasteners to cover windows
- Tarpaulin canvas (tarps) for temporary roof repairs
- Handsaw and/or chainsaw and fuel
- Assorted nails, wood screws
- Hatchet
- Crowbar

SMART SUPPLIES

- Battery-powered camping lantern and flashlights
- Batteries for camping lantern
- Portable camp stove or grill
- Camping potty
- Video or disposable camera
- Smartphone
- Solar lights
- Gas can

- Local and state roadmaps
- Tent
- Games, activities, books to read for children and family members

SPECIAL NEEDS

Some families will need special items added to their disaster list. Examples of these are the following:

- Special foods for special diets
- Extra hearing aid batteries
- Denture care items
- Spare eyeglasses or contact lens supplies
- Baby food, diapers, baby wipes
- Pets: One gallon of water per pet. Leash or pet carrier & pet food.

Pet-Friendly Shelters: Remember that pets are usually not allowed in general shelters. If you live in an evacuation zone where shelters accept pets, you may need to be pre-registered. Make sure you have their I.D. tags and inoculation certificates.

Special Needs Shelters: If you or a family member have a chronic illness or disability, you may have special, even essential survival needs. You may want to know ahead of time if the area you live in has a shelter to accommodate special needs. Preregistration for such services may also be required, so check on both the availability and admission requirements. The shelter may only accept residents with a physical condition requiring medical or nursing care and who cannot be provided for in a general population shelter. In order to be admitted, individuals may need to be able to sleep safely on a cot or mat and meet certain criteria such as needing:

- nursing assistance with medication or medical care
- monitoring of vital signs
- constant electric power for medical equipment

DURING AND AFTER THE DISASTER: *Stay Tuned In!*

- Local media channels are your primary source of information during a disaster. They work with the emergency operation center to provide up-to-date information that can keep you safe.
- Use your battery-operated radio, television or computer to stay informed about weather conditions, hazards, closed roads, curfews and relief center locations.

SAFETY

- Do not use candles. Be extremely careful where fire is concerned.
- Never use a generator or charcoal grill inside your home or inside your garage.
- Most hurricane-related injuries occur after the storm when people are

cleaning up debris. Wear proper safety gear and make sure you know how to properly use power tools and machinery.
- Never work alone. It may be best to hire skilled and insured professionals.

DAMAGES

- List and take photos and/or video footage of any damage to your property or belongings that resulted from the disaster. These will be important to have for your insurance adjuster or for assistance from FEMA.
- Damage after a disaster can be unpredictable. It can take several days and in some cases several weeks to restore power and other essential services. Crews typically begin work as soon as possible to clear roads and restore services. Be patient.
- Remember that everyone in the community is experiencing the same disaster.
- Do not hoard fuel. Be prepared for long lines at the gas station. Keep your cool and be patient!
- Work together.
- Help your neighbor if you can with everyday tasks and supplies.

SPOILED FOOD

Let's assume you just bought a lot of steaks for a party right before some disaster hits, regardless of whether that disaster occurred because of a storm or an old tree collapsed into your living room. Your power went out and everything in your refrigerator or freezer spoiled. Many homeowners insurance policies will cover this loss. Granted, you'll still have to meet your deductible first, but make sure you include lost food in your claim.

EARTHQUAKE SAFETY TIPS

RED CROSS INFORMATION REGARDING EARTHQUAKES

About Earthquakes

An earthquake is a sudden, rapid shaking of the earth caused by the breaking and shifting of rock beneath the earth's surface. Earthquakes strike suddenly, without warning, and they can occur at any time of the year, day or night. Forty-five states and territories in the United States are at moderate to very high risk of earthquakes, and they are located in every region of the country. Learn how to prepare for an earthquake with the following safety tips provided by the American Red Cross.[18]

Are You at Increased Risk from Earthquakes?

Contact your local emergency management office, local American Red Cross, state geological survey or department of natural resources for specific information about your community's risk. However, bear in mind:

- Mobile homes and homes not attached to their foundations are at particular risk during an earthquake.
- Buildings with foundations resting on landfill and other unstable soils

are at increased risk of damage.

Did You Know?

Doorways are no stronger than any other part of a structure so don't rely on them for protection! During an earthquake, get under a sturdy piece of furniture and hold on. It will help shelter you from falling objects that could injure you during an earthquake.

Prepare for an Earthquake

- Become aware of fire evacuation and earthquake safety plans for all of the buildings you occupy regularly.
- Pick safe places in each room of your home, workplace and/or school. A safe place could be under a piece of furniture or against an interior wall away from windows, bookcases or tall furniture that could fall on you.
- Practice "drop, cover and hold on" in each safe place. If you do not have sturdy furniture to hold on to, sit on the floor next to an interior wall and cover your head and neck with your arms.
- Keep a flashlight and sturdy shoes by each person's bed in case the earthquake strikes in the middle of the night.
- Make sure your home is securely anchored to its foundation.
- Bolt and brace water heaters and gas appliances to wall studs.
- Bolt bookcases, china cabinets and other tall furniture to wall studs.
- Hang heavy items, such as pictures and mirrors, away from beds, couches and anywhere people sleep or sit.
- Brace overhead light fixtures.
- Install strong latches or bolts on cabinets. Large or heavy items should be closest to the floor.
- Learn how to shut off the gas valves in your home and keep a wrench handy for that purpose.
- Learn about your area's seismic building standards and land use codes before you begin new construction.
- Keep and maintain an emergency supplies kit in an easy-to-access location.

If You Are Inside When the Shaking Starts...

- Drop, cover and hold on. Move as little as possible.
- If you are in bed, stay there, curl up and hold on. Protect your head with a pillow.
- Stay away from windows to avoid being injured by shattered glass.
- Stay indoors until the shaking stops and you are sure it is safe to exit. When it is, use stairs rather than the elevator in case there are aftershocks, power outages or other damage.

- Be aware that fire alarms and sprinkler systems frequently go off in buildings during an earthquake, even if there is no fire.

If You Are Outside When the Shaking Starts...

- Find a clear spot (away from buildings, power lines, trees, streetlights) and drop to the ground. Stay there until the shaking stops.
- If you are in a vehicle, pull over to a clear location and stop. Avoid bridges, overpasses and power lines if possible. Stay inside with your seatbelt fastened until the shaking stops. Then, drive carefully, avoiding bridges and ramps that may have been damaged.
- If a power line falls on your vehicle, do not get out! Wait for assistance.
- If you are in a mountainous area or near unstable slopes or cliffs, be alert for falling rocks and other debris. Landslides are often triggered by earthquakes.

WHAT TO DO AFTER AN EARTHQUAKE

- After an earthquake, the disaster may continue. Expect and prepare for potential aftershocks, landslides or even a tsunami. Tsunamis are often generated by earthquakes.
- Each time you feel an aftershock, drop, cover and hold on. Aftershocks frequently occur minutes, days, weeks and even months following an earthquake.
- Check yourself for injuries and get First Aid, if necessary, before helping injured or trapped persons.
- Put on long pants, a long-sleeved shirt, sturdy shoes and work gloves to protect against injury from broken objects.
- Look quickly for damage in and around your home and get everyone out if your home is unsafe.
- Listen to a portable, battery-operated or hand-crank radio for updated emergency information and instructions.
- Check the telephones in your home or workplace to see if you can get a dial tone. Make brief calls to report life-threatening emergencies.
- Look for and extinguish small fires. Fire is the most common hazard after an earthquake.
- Clean up spilled medications, bleach, gasoline or other flammable liquids immediately.
- Open closet and cabinet doors carefully as contents may have shifted.
- Help people who require special assistance, such as infants, children and the elderly or disabled.
- Watch out for fallen power lines or broken gas lines and stay out of damaged areas.
- Keep animals under your direct control.

- Stay out of damaged buildings.
- If you were away from home, return only when authorities say it is safe to do so. Use extreme caution and examine walls, floors, doors, staircases and windows to check for damage.
- Be careful when driving after an earthquake and anticipate traffic light outages.

Let Your Family Know You're Safe

If your community has experienced a disaster, register on the American Red Cross website to let your family and friends know you are safe.

You may also call 1-866-GET-INFO FREE to register yourself and your family.

FLORIDA RESOURCES

Changes and Updates in Florida

The following information is provided to Florida policyholders.

The Homeowner Claims Bill of Rights Notice to Policyholders (FLORIDA):

The policyholder has a right to:

1) Receive acknowledgement of their claim within 14 days after the claim was communicated to the insurer.

2) Receive communication from the insurer as to the claim being covered in full, partially covered, or denied, or a written statement that your claim is being investigated, within 30 days after the company receives the policyholders completed proof of loss form.

3) Subject to any dual interest noted in the policy, receive full payment of the claim, the undisputed portion of the claim, or the denial of the claim within 90 days.

4) Free mediation of your disputed claim, offered through the Division of Consumer Services, under most circumstances and subject to certain restrictions.

5) Neutral evaluation of a disputed sinkhole claim if the claim is due to sinkhole damage and is covered under the policy.

6) The availability of assistance with any insurance claim or questions pertaining to the handling of your claim from the Division of Consumer Services. They must provide the direct and toll free number and website of the Division on the notice.

You are advised to:

1) Contact your insurer before entering into any contract for repairs to confirm any managed repair policy provisions or optional preferred vendors;

2) Complete and document any emergency repairs that are necessary to prevent further damage. Keep all receipts and take photographs of the damage before and after any repairs.

3) Carefully read contracts that require out-of-pocket expenses or a fee that is based on a percentage of the insurance proceeds that you will receive for repairing or replacing your property;

4) Confirm that contractors are properly licensed to do business in Florida and check to see if they have any complaints filed against them with

the Department of Business and Professional Regulation. Contractors should also be asked for references from previous clients. To verify a contractor license, call the Florida Department of Business and Professional Regulation at 850-487-1395 or visit http://www.myfloridalicense.com/dbpr/.

5) Require all contractors to provide proof of insurance before starting repairs.

6) Secure your property, turn off gas, water and electricity, and contact the insurance company to provide them a phone number where you can be reached if the damage requires you to leave your home.

FRECKS TOP VIDEO PICS YOU SHOULD WATCH

If you view no other videos or links listed in the book, I encourage you to watch these three videos:

1. The PBS FRONTLINE documentary entitled, "The Storm" about FEMA and other government agencies' reaction and subsequent failure to New Orleans citizens during Hurricane Katrina. This would not be the last time FEMA had been publicly criticized on major disasters. Three other disasters – Floyd, Ike and Sandy were highly criticized as well. Don't depend on them to save you during a disaster. For your own sake, look into this interesting investigation at: http://www.pbs.org/wgbh/pages/frontline/storm/view/.

2. Who can you trust? Apparently you can't trust FEMA's National Flood Insurance Program where engineering reports were falsified so they didn't have to pay money out on flood insurance claims during Hurricane Sandy. View this video at: https://www.youtube.com/watch?v=XxhrWhqg8Cw.

3. My own videos taken of the damages from Hurricane Sandy. Are you ready for the next Sandy and have the right kind of insurance? Even though it was a hurricane, hardly anyone had flood insurance. See this video at: https://youtu.be/Vd58gjX6iDE.

ACKNOWLEDGMENTS

Gratitude is known to make people happier, and even as I was neck deep in disaster areas, I saw how true that was. I wrote this manual just for disaster victims - the millions of you out there who endured, suffered and came out on the other side of disaster. I have been humbled by you, annoyed by you, challenged by you and always inspired. I put all of the work into this book because of *you* and what you have shown me over the decades.

I have been blessed to encounter so many grateful souls, and in doing so, became one myself. I thank everyone who has touched my life and inspired me to write these pages.

This book is for the victims of disasters I have had the experience and the privilege to assist and to all the exceptional first responders who dedicate their lives to helping others: The Red Cross, firefighters, police, National Guard, doctors and nurses, plus the various volunteers. And of course, to all the devoted FEMA inspectors, it has been my honor to know you and consider you as my family.

To Denise Hintz, Robin Martin, Valerie Mellema, Mary Ellen Oakes, Toby Raymond, Marianne Thompson and Jack who were instrumental in publishing this manual...and to my best friend and confidant, who without her encouragement and support, this manual would have remained only an idea.

Mom, I love you and thank you.

ABOUT THE AUTHOR

Author Robert Winter studied psychology in college and owned a California construction firm before spending 25 years as a contract FEMA inspector and three years as a certified building inspector. In 1989, when setting out on his first disaster, his life became a "living adventure." This era changed him to his core. His friends and relatives urged him to write about his experiences. Now, more than twenty years later, he actually did.

Some people are born to protect others, and Robert Winter is one of them. Whether it is A-list celebrities in the midst of Los Angeles and Las Vegas crowds, or regular folks trying to recover from the horrors and destruction of a natural disaster, Frecks is the man for the job. As a three-time world karate champion and third degree black belt, he teaches rape prevention techniques to women and has traveled the country working as a bodyguard, once to a single American flag as part of one of the most famous incidents in professional baseball history.[19] Today, he still remains ready with two bags packed - always prepared to fly into another disaster zone.

Once a commercial diver, he happily dove for abalone among great white sharks, enjoys bungee jumping and spent half a year living in Antarctica diving beneath the polar ice. He received the Antarctica Service Medal from the National Science Foundation and the Antarctica Service Medal by the Department of the Navy for his contributions to exploration. Protector of all he meets, adventurer and friend to many, Robert chose the words, "Help, Hope and Comfort" as his business motto, the same words that best describes his life's work.

§§§

If you enjoyed this book, I am inviting you to leave a review online or wherever you purchased the book. It would be greatly appreciated by me.

NOTES & RESOURCES

1. PBS documentary about local, state and federal governments' handling after the Category 4 Hurricane Katrina disaster can be viewed at: http://www.pbs.org/wgbh/pages/frontline/storm/view/#morelink.

2. Go to FEMA's official website at http://www.fema.gov for disaster planning resources and other useful information for the U.S. public.

3. N.A.D.A. guides provide a wealth of information to value everything from automobiles to motorcycles to mobile homes. Visit their website at: http://www.nadaguides.com.

4. The American Insurance Association provides a general overview of Additional Living Expenses (*ALE*) coverage included in certain homeowners policies. Please visit their website to learn about this important component of insurance at: http://www.www.aiadc.org/.

5. ABC television network's *60 Minutes* broadcast on how Hurricane Sandy victims still haven't received insurance money can be found at: https://youtu.be/XxhrWhqg8Cw.

6. NFIP Flood Insurance Claims Handbook. For information, visit http://www.fema.gov/media-library/assets/documents/6659?id=2184.

7. For information on Increased Cost Of Compliance Coverage, see http://www.fema.gov/media-library/assets/documents/12170?id=3010.

8. http://www.ready.gov/build-a-kit for more information on how to build a disaster supply kit.

9. For information about FEMA's Small Business Administration (SBA) loan program, please visit: https://www.sba.gov/content/disaster-loan-paper-applications.

10. For FEMA's Crisis Counseling Program, go to: https://www.fema.gov/recovery-directorate/crisis-counseling-assistance-training-program.

11. For Disaster Legal Services assistance, please visit the website at: https://www.fema.gov/recovery-directorate/disaster-legal-services-fact-sheet.

12. For information regarding Disaster Unemployment Benefits, please

go to: https://www.fema.gov/recovery-directorate/disaster-unemployment-assistance-fact-sheet.

13. For funeral assistance from FEMA, you can find out more at https://www.fema.gov/media-library/assets/documents/24431.

14. Filing a fraudulent claim with FEMA is serious business. Read more about it at: https://www.fema.gov/news-release/2014/03/17/disaster-fraud-filing-false-claim-fema-felony.

15. For storm damage news footage around the Reno/Gardnerville area in February 2015, visit http://youtu.be/EytBGWY35kE.

16. Visit http://dustinthewindFEMAbook.com/ for the author's official website and blog, including travel tips (Smell the Roses).

17. The Red Cross store offers a hand crank radio for disaster preparedness at: http://www.redcrossstore.org/item/ARCPT300W.

18. Visit the Red Cross website for information on earthquakes along with just about any other natural disaster you can imagine, including volcanoes! Go to: http://www.redcross.org/prepare/disaster/earthquake.

19. Known as one of the greatest plays in baseball history, Rick Monday's historic April 25, 1976 'saving the American flag' at Dodgers Stadium during the American Bicentennial can be viewed online at: https://www.youtube.com/watch?v=IrV8QPQAhxo&feature=youtu.be. Thirty years later, this author served as its bodyguard during the *Patriot Guard Riders* tour across the country.

20. Visit: http://celebrities4disasterrelief.org/ for more about the Robert Winter's disaster relief donation site.

21. Email Robert at: Femadude15@aol.com.

22. Go to Twitter at: https://twitter.com/@DustInTheWindBk to read daily tips about disaster preparedness and other related info.

23. YouTube chronicles Robert's other exploits. Visit him at: http://www.youtube.com/results?search_query=FRECKSZONE to know more about the crazy, wild things the author does in his free time.

CHECKLISTS

CHECKLIST FOR ITEMS THAT NEED TO BE ADDRESSED BY THE FEMA INSPECTOR

If an item is not on this list, more than likely FEMA does not cover it under its essential needs program, but never hesitate to ask the inspector.

Every disaster is different with some items that FEMA will cover. These items vary from state to state and from disaster to disaster.

1. Furnace
2. Hot water heater
3. Central air/thermostat, air conditioner (window)
4. Heat pump
5. Ducting (A/C, heating)
6. Sewer or septic tank , drain field
7. Well/pump house, pumps
8. Power pole
9. Electrical weather head
10. Gas meter/piping, propane tank, meter, etc.
11. Water line/piping/plumbing items
12. Electric meter/breakers/fuses
13. All electric components inundated by water, especially salt water
14. Floors: carpet, wood, vinyl, tile
15. Doors/windows
16. Drywall/paint
17. Insulation/walls, floor, ceiling
18. Exterior wall covering
19. Porch access: stairs, steps, handrails
20. Chimney, fireplace, wood burning stove
21. Foundation, slab, crawl space, basement
22. Roofing
23. Roads, bridges, private access
24. Automobile, motorcycle, transportation
25. Refrigerator, stove, freezer, kitchen table
26. Washer/dryer
27. Furniture, beds, couches, tables, lamps, etc.
28. Radios, television, stereo, electronics, fans
29. Clothing if contaminated by water, destroyed or blown away

30. Toiletries, towels, soap, wash cloths
31. Cabinets/kitchen, bathroom, etc.
32. Sinks, toilets, shower, faucets
33. Debris removal, tree removal, etc.
34. Clean/sanitize property of flood waters
35. Computer if used for work or school
36. Miscellaneous expenses: funeral, dental, medical, moving/storage
37. Number of occupied bedrooms
38. Outbuildings with essential items located inside them

Have these on hand:

1. Receipts for any repairs or replacement of essential need items
2. Receipts of any kind that are storm-related purchases

Know that the inspector is limited to 5 photos total of all damages.

BE FRECKS SMART!

If it's not on the list above, more than likely FEMA does NOT cover those items under its Essential Needs Program. However, never hesitate to ask the inspector whether something is covered or not.

Every disaster is different on some of the items that FEMA will cover under their program. These items can change from state to state and from disaster to disaster.

Remember, NO luxury times are included on this list of essential items and will not be covered under their guidelines (dishwashers, garbage disposals, swimming pools, etc.).

FRECKS TOP 15 CHECKLIST

1. Buy insurance or if you have insurance, meet with your insurance agent and go over all of your coverage including scenarios of disasters in your area.
2. Fill out insurance itemized household list.
3. Before you clean up after a disaster, photograph/video before, during and after clean up.
4. Before you begin repairs, take interior/exterior photographs/video before, during and after repairs.
5. Photograph/video water line damage of flooding using a current newspaper with the date of the newspaper clearly showing.
6. Study Frecks' Table on page 18 to determine when to call FEMA or your insurance company.
7. With depreciation, make sure your damages are two to three times higher than your deductible on your insurance policy.
8. Receipts, Receipts, Receipts! Save every single receipt no matter insignificant for proof of purchases for FEMA, the insurance company and the IRS.
9. Have a disaster plan and survival kit.
10. Get a public adjuster if you're not happy with the offer from your insurance company.
11. Not happy with your FEMA assistance? File an appeal letter.
12. On a federally declared disaster, it's worth a visit to the (DRC) Disaster Recovery Center.
13. If you're denied by FEMA and your insurance company, apply for a low interest SBA loan.
14. Make sure your FEMA inspector and insurance adjuster inspect the entire interior and exterior of your home including the roof, basement, crawl space and any outbuildings.
15. Make sure you know whether your FEMA inspector and/or storm adjuster are experienced. It will make all the difference to your financial disaster recovery.

Preparedness is one of the most important things you can do to save lives and property.

Next is the Insurance Household Inventory Checklist for you to walk through your property and check off the items, filling in other important information. You can always make additional copies before writing on them and use to update your records annually. Keep this checklist current.

I placed these in the back of the book for you to tear out easily, so use them, please! THIS IS VERY IMPORTANT if you want to have a disaster claim completed as soon as possible. It makes the adjuster's job very easy because these are the exact same sheets he or she will hand you after a disaster to complete again after your household items are destroyed or thrown out.

Living Room			
Item and Description	Brand/Serial No.	When Bought	Price Paid
Carpet/rugs			
Curtains/drapes/wooden shutters/blinds			
Sofa			
Loveseat/chaise lounge			
Chairs			
Coffee tables/sofa table			
End tables			
Desk			
Pictures & other wall hangings			
Bookcases			
Books			
Clocks			
Lamps			
Entertainment center/satellite radio			
Television/plasma/HD			
VCR/DVD/DVR			
Camcorder			
CD Player			
Stereos/Bose system			
Radios/MP3 player			
Records/tapes/CD's/DVD's			
Desk			
Mirrors			
Vases			
Plants/planters			
Fireplace equipment			
Coin collection			
Stamp collection			
Portable air conditioner			
Other			
Sub-Total			

Dining Room			
Item and Description	Brand/Serial No.	When Bought	Price Paid
Carpet/rugs			
Curtains/drapes/wooden shutters/blinds			
Buffet			
Table/formal dining set			
Chairs			
China cabinet/curio cabinet			
China			
Silverware			
Crystal/silver serving dishes			
Tablecloths & napkins			
Tea or coffee set			
Serving table/cart			
Clocks			
Lamps/fixtures			
Wall hangings			
Portable air conditioner			
Other			
Sub-Total			

Bathroom 1			
Item and Description	Brand/Serial No.	When Bought	Price Paid
Clothes hamper			
Curtains/drapes/wooden shutters/blinds			
Electrical appliances			
Scale			
Shower curtains			
Linens			
Toilet articles			
Pictures			
Other			
Sub-Total			

Bathroom 2			
Item and Description	Brand/Serial No.	When Bought	Price Paid
Clothes hamper			
Curtains/drapes/wooden shutters/blinds			
Electrical appliances			
Scale			
Shower curtains			
Linens			
Toilet articles			
Pictures			
Other			
Sub-Total			

Bedroom 1			
Item and Description	Brand/Serial No.	When Bought	Price Paid
Carpet/rugs			
Curtains/drapes/wooden shutters/blinds			
Headboards			
Mattresses			
Box springs			
Dressers			
Chests			
Dressing tables			
Nightstands			
Lamps			
Mirrors			
Clocks			
Radio/satellite radio/Bose system			
Television/plasma			
Sewing machine			
Wall hangings			
Clothing			
Jewelry			
Furs			
Money			
Bookcases			
Books			
Portable air conditioner			
Chairs			
Desk			
Other			
Sub-Total			

Bedroom 2			
Item and Description	Brand/Serial No.	When Bought	Price Paid
Carpet/rugs			
Curtains/drapes/wooden shutters/blinds			
Headboards			
Mattresses			
Box springs			
Dressers			
Chests			
Dressing tables			
Nightstands			
Lamps			
Mirrors			
Clocks			
Radio/satellite radio/Bose system			
Television/plasma			
Sewing machine			
Wall hangings			
Clothing			
Jewelry			
Furs			
Money			
Bookcases			
Books			
Portable air conditioner			
Chairs			
Desk			
Other			
Sub-Total			

Home Office			
Item and Description	Brand/Serial No.	When Bought	Price Paid
Desk			
Chair			
Couch			
Computer			
Printer			
Scanner			
Fax machine			
Answering machine			
Cordless phone			
Tape recorder			
Securities			
Manuscripts			
Business property			
Camera/digital			
Bookcases			
Books			
Curtains/drapes/ wooden shutters/blinds			
Table			
Lamps			
Radios/satellite radio/ Bose system			
Rugs			
Fireplace equipment			
Portable air conditioner			
Other			
Sub-Total			

Kitchen			
Item and Description	Brand/Serial No.	When Bought	Price Paid
Table			
Chairs			
Cabinets			
Lights			
Curtains/drapes/wooden shutters/blinds			
Refrigerator			
Freezer			
Stove			
Microwave oven			
Convection oven			
Dishwasher			
Disposal unit			
Washer			
Dryer			
Food processor			
Small appliances			
Pots/pans			
Bowls			
Dishes			
Glasses			
Kitchen tools			
Utensils			
Pictures			
Clocks			
Television			
Radio			
Step stool			
Food supplies			
Other			
Sub -Total			

Garage/Basement/Attic			
Item and Description	Brand/Serial No.	When Bought	Price Paid
Furniture			
Luggage/trunks			
Sports equipment			
Toys/games			
Boats			
Trailers			
Heater			
Dehumidifier			
Ornamental lawn items			
Lawn mower/weed trimmer			
Shovel			
Spreaders			
Sprinklers/hoses			
Snow blower			
Garden tools/supplies			
Ladders/step stool			
Work bench			
Carpentry tools/supplies			
Holiday decorations			
Canned foods/supplies			
Pet supplies			
Other			
Sub-Total			

Porch/Patio			
Item and Description	Brand/Serial No.	When Bought	Price Paid
Chairs			
Tables			
Umbrella			
Floor covering			
Outdoor cooking equipment			
Plant/planters			
Other			
Sub-Total			
GRAND TOTAL			

Made in the USA
Monee, IL
04 November 2026

67380511R00081